RAILS OVER THE MOUNTAINS

RAILS OVER THE MOUNTAINS

EXPLORING THE RAILWAY
HERITAGE OF CANADA'S
WESTERN MOUNTAINS

RON BROWN

DUNDURN
TORONTO

Editor: Dominic Farrell
Design: Courtney Horner
Cover image: Ron Brown
Printer: Webcom

Library and Archives Canada Cataloguing in Publication

Brown, Ron, 1945-, author
Rails over the mountains : exploring the railway heritage of Canada's western mountains / Ron Brown.

Includes bibliographical references and index.
Issued in print and electronic formats.
ISBN 978-1-4597-3359-6 (paperback).--ISBN 978-1-4597-3358-9 (pdf).--
ISBN 978-1-4597-3357-2 (epub)

1. Railroads--Canada, Western--History. 2. Canada, Western--History.
I. Title.

HE2809.B76 2016   385.09712   C2016-901746-X
                                             C2016-901747-8

1 2 3 4 5   20 19 18 17 16

We acknowledge the support of the **Canada Council for the Arts** and the **Ontario Arts Council** for our publishing program. We also acknowledge the financial support of the **Government of Canada** through the **Canada Book Fund** and **Livres Canada Books**, and the **Government of Ontario** through the **Ontario Book Publishing Tax Credit** and the **Ontario Media Development Corporation**.

Care has been taken to trace the ownership of copyright material used in this book. The author and the publisher welcome any information enabling them to rectify any references or credits in subsequent editions.
— *J. Kirk Howard, President*

The publisher is not responsible for websites or their content unless they are owned by the publisher.

Printed and bound in Canada.

Visit us at
Dundurn.com
@dundurnpress
Facebook.com/dundurnpress
Pinterest.com/dundurnpress

Dundurn
3 Church Street, Suite 500
Toronto, Ontario, Canada
M5E 1M2

CONTENTS

ACKNOWLEDGEMENTS

Although my research for this book happened with minimal assistance, I would nonetheless like to extend my appreciation to those who did assist. They include the knowledgeable media contacts at the Fairmont Banff Springs Hotel, Hotel Vancouver, the Met Hotel in New Westminster, Vernon Tourism, Victoria Tourism, and Kelowna Tourism.

Thank you to the staff and curators at the fabulous Canadian Museum of Rail Travel in Cranbrook, the Revelstoke Railway Museum, the Kamloops Heritage Railway, the West Coast Heritage Railway in Squamish, the Kettle Valley Steam Railway in Summerland, and the Pemberton Museum, all of whom provided tours and vital information.

VIA Rail Canada, the *Rocky Mountaineer*, and Parks Canada all generously shared their images with me. Thanks also to HelloBC for providing me with a free road map and accommodation guide.

For their help with the preparation and promotion of the book, my thanks go to Dundurn publisher, Kirk Howard, and his fine staff, including my mentor Margaret Bryant, my publicist Jaclyn Hodsdon, my editor Dominic Farrell, and Cheryl Hawley. Any errors which remain are on me.

INTRODUCTION

This volume completes my cross-country odyssey along Canada's rail lines, both past and present.[*] Our railway history began in Nova Scotia with the coal mines of Cape Breton and the railways that served them. The journey continued with the tracks into the growing colonies of Nova Scotia, New Brunswick, Ontario, and Quebec. Companies like the Grand Trunk and the Intercolonial Railways provided the key routes, while local lines served as branches. Then came John A. Macdonald, with his grand "national dream" of linking the new country from coast to coast with a rail line. The completion of the Canadian Pacific Railway (CPR) in 1885 opened up vast stretches of the Prairies and breached the mountain barriers of western Alberta and British Columbia.

The greatest challenge that confronted the builders of these lines was how to breach the mountain barriers that loomed above them at the western end of the Prairies. Passes had to be found, tunnels and bridges built, town sites located, and workers transported and lodged.

In the following decades, those labourers would build two more transcontinental rail lines in addition to the Canadian Pacific Railway, namely, the Canadian Northern Railway (CNoR) and the Grand Trunk Pacific (GTP)/National Transcontinental Railway (NTR). As the tracks unrolled, more lines entered Canada's resource-rich regions of northern Quebec, northern Ontario, British Columbia, and Alberta. American rivals slipped in from across the border.

With the tracks in place, grand stations appeared in towns and cities. As with the classical temples in the Roman and Greek cities that inspired them, their arches and pillars signalled to arriving and departing travellers alike that the stations were the grand entranceways to urban Canada. The CPR and CNoR stations in Vancouver exemplify this approach. The railways wanted it known what their status was, and so they built grand temples to demonstrate that to the people.

Much of Canada's heritage legacy has evolved around the railways and their effect on the landscape. Wonderful chateau-style hotels rose in the mountains

* Beginning with *Rails to the Atlantic, Rails Across Ontario,* and *Rails Across the Prairies.*

and cities. Stations often mimicked that architectural style as well, as shown in the old CPR station in New Westminster, B.C. Rustic stations of log reflected the natural attractions of the mountains.

Most stations, however, were purely functional. Appearing at fifteen-kilometre intervals along the lines, they offered ticketing, freight shipment, and a wire-news service to the local communities. Water towers for the boilers in the steam engines usually appeared at alternate station sites. Station agents found living space in the stations themselves, whether in second-floor living quarters, or simply in an apartment tucked into a rooftop dormer. Divisional points at 150-kilometre intervals supplied the railway with their operational needs, such as bunkhouses for train crews, larger homes for management, roundhouses, sorting yards, as well as coaling and sanding facilities.

Even during the Great Depression, railways retained their essential role. Everything went by rail ... livestock, grain, farm products, coal, logs, and most minerals. Since air travel was still in its infancy, the railways continued to carry travellers to school, to lakeside retreats, and even to world-renowned tourist destinations, in particular the much-promoted Rocky Mountains.

While the needs of carrying military personnel during the Second World War handed the railways their greatest-ever passenger loads, trouble was on the horizon. With the end of the bloodshed and the bombing, a new era was dawning: the Auto Age. Families began to acquire cars and, increasingly, they found more convenient ways to get around. No more freezing on a windy platform. Highways improved. Trucks took over from freight trains. Buses replaced tramcars, and diesel-powered locomotives replaced steam locomotives. Stations closed and were demolished, as were the water towers that stood near them. Divisional points were eliminated. Roundhouses and coal docks disappeared from the railway landscapes. Crew quarters required more modern and efficient conveniences, and so new facilities were built to replace the drafty old wooden bunkhouses.

Local freight service gave way to kilometre-long unit trains, while short-sighted governments eliminated vital passenger services. Tracks were lifted, leaving bare gravel roadbeds, many of which disappeared into the hands of adjacent property owners.

Had Canada's railway legacy ended?

In the early 1980s, thanks to an ill-advised public relations fiasco with the CPR, Canadians awakened to the plight of that heritage. In 1982, the CPR clandestinely destroyed the much-loved West Toronto CPR station. The outrage that followed led to the creation of a unique piece of federal legislation known as the Heritage Railway Stations Protection Act (the HRSPA). Passed in a rare unanimous vote in the House of Commons, the law has allowed the minister of the environment to designate and protect important railway stations across the country. Many of those saved have become restaurants, bars, and offices. Others have become railway museums.

But much of the railway landscape remained unprotected. Of the more than one hundred roundhouses that actually survived "dieselization" in western Canada, nearly all were removed. Their purpose-built form and distant locations in the rail yards often made repurposing them unfeasible. Water towers and coal docks had no future either and could not be saved.

Still, Canadians were becoming increasingly aware of a legacy they were on the verge of losing. Endangered stations were relocated to become museums. Railway enthusiasts began assembling rolling stock, saving it from the scrapyard. In many cases, the old railway hotels were renovated, with their rail roots in mind. In fact, some of North America's grandest hotels, the Banff Springs, the Chateau Lake Louise, the Hotel Vancouver, and the Empress Hotel in Victoria all reflect their deep railway roots. Tour trains began to retrace the routes of the early railway journeys.

Looking back today, Canada can be proud of the railway legacy that many have worked hard to retain. And throughout the mountains of western Canada that work is readily evident.

Rail museums in Squamish, Revelstoke, Prince George, and Cranbrook vie with the best on the continent. VIA Rail, the *Rocky Mountaineer*, and the *Royal Canadian Pacific* offer spectacular journeys through spectacular scenery. Local tour trains have kept alive the steam train era in places like Summerland, B.C., Fort Steele, Alberta, and Port Alberni on Vancouver Island. Historic wooden trestles and dark tunnels are protected in places like the Othello Tunnels near Hope, B.C., the Myra Canyon Trestles near Kelowna, and the Kinsol Trestle near Duncan, B.C.

Countless books and websites also keep alive the railway era and tell of an undying love in Canada for what is one of the country's most important legacies.

THE CANADIAN RAILWAY HALL OF FAME

Unlike the North America Railway Hall of Fame, which is situated in the grand old Canada Southern Railway station in St. Thomas, ON, (Canada's "railway city"), the Canadian Railway Hall of Fame is strictly web-based.

This ensures its accessibility to everyone with a computer, regardless of where they live. Inaugurated in 2002, the virtual museum features categories such as "Leaders," "Heroes," "Communities," and "Technology." And western Canada's mountains play a prominent role in the hall.

The website's first inductees included, Sir William Cornelius Van Horne, George Stephen (aka Lord Mount Stephen), and Donald Smith (aka Lord Strathcona), builders of the CPR; Sir William Mackenzie and Sir Donald Mann, who cobbled together the Canadian Northern Railway; James J. Hill of the Great Northern Railway; and Charles Melville Hays who promoted the Grand Trunk Pacific Railway. All were pre-eminent in the creation of the railway network that crossed Canada's western mountains. The western Canadian communities inducted into the hall include Banff, Alberta, Revelstoke, B.C., and Craigellachie, B.C., the site of the famous CPR "Last Spike." Engineering accomplishments celebrated in the hall include the Myra Canyon Trestles and the Mount Macdonald Tunnel. According to the hall's website (railfame.ca), any individual or organization may nominate an inductee.

This book, as with the others in the series, offers readers an opportunity to relive the railway roots of Canada's western mountains. The sites listed are all accessible to the public (unless otherwise stated), and directions to them are included. The interested reader will need little more than a provincial highway map or, better still, a road atlas. Google maps and Google StreetView are useful references as well. The Bibliography lists books and websites that I have sourced, and which complement and enlarge on the material in the book. Many link to local history sites, museum sites, and government heritage sites.

THE RAILS ARRIVE

1

While the CPR's "national dream" has become a legend in book and song, Canada, in fact, saw the fulfillment of three "national dreams." The first, of course, was that of the CPR. As part of its agreement with the colony of British Columbia to enter Confederation, the Government of Canada chartered the Canadian Pacific Railway to construct a rail line from the east to the coast of British Columbia. Train travel along the new line began in 1886. Some two decades later, the Canadian Northern Railway began operation. For this, the railway building duo of William Mackenzie and Donald Mann, later knighted, cobbled together a trans-Canada rail network from Nova Scotia to Vancouver. A short while later, Prime Minister Sir Wilfrid Laurier decided that Canada needed a third rail line, the Grand Trunk Pacific.

Each of these faced the same huge hurdles. After pushing the tracks across the comparatively easy-to-overcome terrain of the Canadian Prairies, the railway builders came up against the mountains of the West. First came the Rocky Mountains, then came the Purcells, then the Columbia Mountains, with the Selkirk and all of its other ranges, including the Monashee Mountains; then there followed the Thompson Plateau and the Cascade Mountains; and after all that, there was the Coast Range. Between all of these hurdles were a series of river valleys oriented in a north-south direction. In order to keep the track gradients manageable, the rail lines tended to closely follow these valleys. But that often meant that the routes were circuitous, and even then had to cross steep canyons or tunnel through the mountains themselves. By the time the flurry of track laying finally ended, Canada found itself with three main lines through the mountains, and connecting links, as well as some U.S.-based intruders from across the border.

THE RAILWAY BUILDERS

William Cornelius Van Horne

Born in 1843, Van Horne cut his railway teeth working in the telegraph office of the Illinois Central Railroad in Joliet. He worked his way up to ticket agent and then in 1872 became divisional superintendent on the Chicago

& Alton Railroad. In 1880 he met James J. Hill, who had signed a contract with the Canadian government to build a rail line across the country to be known as the Canadian Pacific Railway. He recommended that Van Horne be hired to manage the line's construction. Van Horne was always out front with his comments, promising that he could build the prairie portion of the railway within a single year, 1882, which he did. Following the driving of the last spike in 1885, Van Horne became the CPR's general manager.

One of his key decisions during construction was to redirect the line's route from the Yellowhead Pass farther north to the Kicking Horse Pass in the southern Rockies. Here he again encountered Hill, who was promoting the incursion of his Northern Pacific Railway into southern British Columbia and Alberta. To counter the incursion from his old friend, in 1896 Van Horne secured funding from the government to build a southern main line through the Crowsnest Pass in southern Alberta.

Along his main line, Van Horne put his savvy to work by sending simple station plans, later nicknamed the "Van Hornes," to local contractors to get the line running as quickly as possible. He also promoted the scenic Rocky Mountains as a tourist attraction by ordering the building of glamorous hotels and dining stations. To ensure this scenery would remain unspoiled, he convinced the Canadian government to enact laws to create national parks at Yoho and Banff.

Following the completion of the CPR, Van Horne spread his talents to resource development and to railway building in Cuba. His legacy lives on not just in the story of the CPR but in the preservation of two of his grand properties, a house in Montreal and an ocean-side retreat in New Brunswick known as Ministers Island. Van Horne died in 1915 and was buried back home in Joliet.

Charles Melville Hays

Born in 1856 in Illinois, Hays, like Van Horne, got an early start in the railway business, beginning at age seventeen in the ticket office of the Atlantic and Pacific Railroad. By 1887, he was the general manager of the Wabash Western Railway. In 1896 he moved to Montreal, and by 1909 was president of the Grand Trunk Railway. He went on to promote the development of the Grand Trunk Pacific Railway (GTP), a route from Winnipeg to Prince Rupert that would link up with the government's National Transcontinental Railway. Later, after travelling to England to secure funding for the GTP, he perished on the return journey on the ill-fated *Titanic*.

Despite Hays's efforts, the rail line lacked the financial resources to overcome the needs, both material and financial, of the First World War, and the GTP was assumed by the newly created government railway, the Canadian National Railway. His legacy lives on in such hotels as the Chateau Laurier and in the name of Melville, SK, a key GTP town on the Prairies.

William Mackenzie and Donald Mann: The CNoR's Dynamic Duo

William Mackenzie, raised in Kirkfield, ON, joined his brothers' contracting company and was soon supplying timber to a variety of Ontario rail lines. With the start of the CPR construction, Mackenzie was hired to supply timber for the construction of trestles and stations for that national enterprise. In 1879, his future partner, Donald Mann, left the Methodist ministry to enter the lumber business. He was put in charge of barging the West's first steam locomotive to Winnipeg and soon began working for the CPR. Here, his grading and earth-moving contracts soon put him in touch with William Mackenzie. The two joined forces and began to make a name for themselves as railway builders.

In 1897, they launched their unparalleled railway-building empire when they acquired the Lake Manitoba Railway and Canal Company, then bankrupt. In 1899, they formed the Canadian Northern Railway and began buying up bankrupt lines or unused charters, and soon began to cobble together a nation-wide rail network. In 1905, they began to expand westward, reaching Edmonton in 1910. In 1911, they acquired a townsite at Port Mann on the B.C. coast, where they proposed to locate their car shops. But with land values in decline, they instead joined their railway with B.C.'s Great Northern Railway and so extended the line directly to Vancouver instead. There they built one of western Canada's finest neo-classical stations.

Sadly, by 1915, with the First World War taking up virtually all of the government's financing, Mackenzie and Mann had overextended themselves and the line was bankrupt. Like the GTP, it would become part of the new Canadian National Railway. While Mackenzie's home still stands in Kirkfield, ON, that of Donald Mann, a mansion named Fallingbrook was destroyed by fire. Only the gatehouse still stands, on Toronto's Kingston Road east of Fallingbrook Avenue.

Andrew McCulloch: The KVR "Wonder"

After graduating with a business degree in Kingston, ON, in 1888, McCulloch moved west to work on the Great Northern Railway. After a career that included work on a variety of rail lines, such as the GTP, the Columbia & Western (C&W), and the Kaslo and Slocan railways, he was appointed chief engineer by the CPR in 1910 to solve the challenges facing the construction of the Kettle Valley Railway.

The most daunting of these were the Myra and Coquihalla canyons. The Myra Canyon, which rises one thousand metres above the Okanagan lowlands, necessitated the building of a series of eighteen trestles in order to allow tracks to be laid around the amphitheatre-like canyon. In order to overcome the steep vertical cliffs that close in on the Coquihalla Canyon, McCulloch and his surveyors needed to devise an even more extreme solution. First, in order to take the measurements of the canyon, they had to descend the cliff in wicker baskets. Once the canyon's measurements had been calculated, McCulloch and his team blasted a series of four tunnels through the hard granite of the twisting canyon walls. Both sites are now part of provincial parks. Lauded for his feats of engineering, which have been labelled "McCulloch's Wonder," Andrew McCulloch died in 1945 and is buried in Lakeview Cemetery in Penticton. His grave marker lies in section D, near the cemetery's main entrance.

Robert Dunsmuir

Had it not been for Robert Dunsmuir, Vancouver Island might never have had a rail line. In 1850, Robert Dunsmuir arrived from Scotland and joined the

Hudson's Bay Company, moving to Vancouver Island to work as an overman at the company's coal mine near Fort Rupert. After being transferred to Nanaimo, in 1853 he became the resident manager of the Harewood Coal Company. He soon built his own colliery, which was to become British Columbia's largest.

In 1882, the contract to build the CPR's Vancouver Island link was put out for tender, and Dunsmuir, along with Lewis Clement, chief engineer of the Atlantic and Pacific Railway, competed for it. Although Clement first received the nod, his financing fell through and Dunsmuir won the day. Construction was finished in April 1886 when Prime Minister Sir John A. Macdonald drove in the last spike at Cliffside. The railway was called the Esquimalt, for the area of the naval base where its southern terminal lay, and Nanaimo Railway.

Dunsmuir died in 1886 shortly after. Macdonald had driven in the E&N's last spike. In 1905, Dunsmuir's son James sold the line to the CPR, which operated it until 1999 when the CPR in turn sold the line to RailAmerica. Dunsmuir's grand Victorian mansion, Craigdarroch Castle, still stands and is today a National Historic Site.

THE RAILWAYS

The Canadian Pacific Railway:
Sir John A. Macdonald's "National Dream"

Sir John A. Macdonald never used the term "national dream" for the idea of a railway spanning the country from coast to coast, but it surely was his wish.

It all began in 1871 when the prime minister promised that as a condition of British Columbia joining his cherished Confederation, he would promise them a railway link to the east. However a political scandal and election defeat set back the start of construction until 1881.

Construction across the Prairies went quickly and easily. But the mountain barriers proved a more difficult challenge. The first route that caught the CPR's eye was through the Yellowhead Pass, which had fewer steep grades to deal with than did some of the other obvious routes. However, the railway opted instead for a route farther south, one through Kicking Horse Pass and Rogers Pass. This option meant a shorter route and one which would better compete with the American rail lines threatening to enter the country from the south. However, it also meant greater engineering challenges. Mountains had to be circumvented or burrowed through and deep chasms had to be bridged. Steep grades meant slower train movement, and heavy snowfalls posed an ongoing threat of avalanches resulting in a series of snow sheds.

Because passenger trains could not haul their heavy dining cars over the steep grades, especially the one east of Field known as the "Big Hill," which had a slope of 4.4 percent, the CPR built a series of dining hotels, which in themselves became popular tourist destinations. The famous "Spiral Tunnels" built in 1909 helped reduce the grade from more than 4.4 percent to 2.2 percent. However, deadly avalanches underscored the urgency of more snow sheds and tunnels, and in 1916, the Connaught Tunnel opened, bypassing the dangerous Rogers Pass route. It also helped to reduce the gradient even further. So did the Mount Macdonald Tunnel, which opened in 1988, becoming North America's longest tunnel and an engineering marvel in its own right.

DRIVING OF THE LAST SPIKE - CANADIAN PACIFIC RAILWAY
CRAIGELLACHIE, BRITISH COLUMBIA, NOVEMBER 7, 1885

This iconic image of the CPR's last spike is displayed at the Craigellachie National Historic Site in British Columbia.

As the train crews were inching westward, a separate gang was heading eastward. Andrew Onderdonk was moving his crews eastward from Savona. Finally, the two met up in a mountain pass at a place called Craigellachie. Here, on November 7, 1885, a collection of CPR dignitaries stepped off the train and posed for the camera. In a now iconic image by Winnipeg photographer Alexander Ross, Donald Smith, the CPR's president, can be seen hammering in the last spike. (Or trying to. The first effort bent the spike and Smith had to try again. The second time around he was successful.)

In 1886, the summer after that photograph was taken, the first train arrived en route to Port Moody, the first terminus. The next year came the first passenger train to arrive in the eventual terminus at Vancouver.

This historic poster in the Yaletown roundhouse display depicts the arrival of CPR # 374, the first steam engine to reach Vancouver's new terminal.

The CPR's last spike site has become a National Historic Site, and popular tourist stop on the Trans-Canada Highway as well as on the *Rocky Mountaineer* tour train. Here a cairn with historic images stands by the tracks in the shadow of a caboose. A gift shop and another building recreate the station styles of the day.

Here too is a tribute to the Chinese workers who toiled under demeaning and treacherous conditions to

The historic Last Spike cairn is flanked by a caboose at Craigellachie.

help Canada complete its line. One worker in four lost his life to falls or explosions, yet the Chinese workers received only a fraction of the pay given to white workers. Poor living conditions also took a great toll. In later years, Chinese Canadian residents were discriminated against even more severely by the infamous "head" tax, and being denied the right to sponsor their family members.

In 1989, the Memorial to Commemorate the Chinese Railroad Workers in Canada was unveiled in Toronto, appropriately located beside the railway tracks near the Rogers Centre. Created by Eldon Garnet and Francis LeBouthillier, the inscription reads:

> *Dedicated to the Chinese railroad workers who helped construct the Canadian Pacific Railway through the Rocky Mountains of Alberta and British Columbia thus uniting Canada geographically and politically.*
>
> *From 1880 to 1885 seventeen thousand men from the province of Kwangtung (Guangdong), China,*

going back to China when their labour was no longer needed, thousands drifted in near destitution along the completed track. All of them remained nameless in the history of Canada.

We erect this monument to remember them.

The touching monument to the conditions faced by Chinese labourers in building the CPR overlooks the rail yards in Toronto.

came to work on the Western section of the railway through the treacherous terrain of the Canadian Rockies. Far from their families, amid hostile sentiments, these men laboured long hours and made the completion of the railway physically and economically possible.

More than four thousand Chinese workers lost their lives during construction. With no means of

In 2006, the Government of Canada issued a full parliamentary apology for its deplorable treatment of these hard-working men.

The Esquimalt and Nanaimo Railway (E&N)

Incorporated in 1883, the E&N on Vancouver Island was to be the final link in Macdonald's transcontinental line to the Pacific. However, crossing the Strait of Georgia from the mainland would prove to be insurmountable, and so the CPR was terminated at first in Port Moody and then Vancouver. Initiated by coal baron Robert Dunsmuir, the E&N would end up being the island's main line.

By 1884, the line had been built from the naval base at Esquimalt, across the harbour from Victoria, for 115 kilometres to the port of Nanaimo. Four years later, it was extended into Victoria itself. In 1905, under CPR ownership, the E&N was extended to Courtenay, Port Alberni, and Lake Cowichan. At its peak, the line extended nearly three hundred kilometres (210 miles) and contained more than fifty stations. The line contained some of North America's highest railway bridges and trestles, such as that over the Niagara Canyon. On August 13, 1886, Macdonald drove in the last spike at Cliffside station near Shawnigan Lake.

The Crowsnest Pass in the southern Rockies was another early route used by the CPR to conquer the mountain range.

In the 1950s, the CPR began to cut back its operations, closing the Lake Cowichan line. In 1953, the CPR ended passenger service to Port Alberni and in 1998 sold the Port Alberni branch line to RailAmerica, which switched to trucking shortly thereafter, although tracks remain and a short section near Port Alberni hosts a tour train. The main line however has not seen trains since 2011, when track conditions were deemed questionable. Public pressure since then has kept open the possibility of rail service being resumed.

The Kettle Valley Railway (KVR): McCulloch's Wonder

That this railway got built at all is indeed a "wonder." Desperate to complete its southern main line to the coast, the CPR's Van Horne began a route from Lethbridge in southern Alberta through the Crowsnest Pass in the Rocky Mountains to a location called Midway. From there he hired Andrew McCulloch to finish the route from Midway to the CPR main line at Hope. This would become the legendary Kettle Valley Railway. But to complete this railway, it would be necessary to overcome some astonishing engineering hurdles.

First there was the Myra Canyon, which soared more than one thousand metres above the Okanagan Valley and required eighteen trestles. The steep, formidable Coquihalla Canyon required a series of four tunnels and bridges along the foaming river in the Coquihalla Canyon. By the time it opened in 1915, the railway had been appropriately dubbed "McCulloch's Wonder."

From Princeton to Brookmere, the KVR shared rights with the Great Northern Railway which had already constructed that section of the line and whose last spike was driven at Brookmere. The KVR's last spike was driven by the Tullameen River bridge in East Princeton, a bridge nicknamed the "Bridge of Dreams" by the railway workers. Today that bridge has been rebuilt and is now an award-winning link on the popular Kettle Valley Rail Trail.

The section of track from Spences Bridge on the CPR's main line to Brookmere actually predated the completion of the KVR to Hope, having been started in 1907 to connect with the CPR at Merritt in 1915. In the end, all track became part of the CPR's southern main-line network. But by 1961 the Coquihalla portion from Brookmere to Hope had proved too much to maintain and the CPR rerouted its traffic northward from Brookmere to Spences Bridge. The length of the KVR from Midway to Hope stretched 260 kilometres and from Midway to Spences Bridge roughly 285 kilometres. The section from Brookmere to Hope closed in 1960, then to Spences Bridge in 1990. By then, the KVR had seen its last trains, and from Castlegar to Spences Bridge the CPR southern main line fell silent.

The Grand Trunk Pacific Railway (GTP)

This line was an extension of another "national dream," that of Prime Minister Sir Wilfrid Laurier. When the Canadian government built the National Transcontinental Railway from Moncton, NB, to Winnipeg, it fully expected the Grand Trunk Railway to build and operate the line from there to a port on the Pacific coast, namely Port Simpson (now known as Lax Kw'alaams) near the contentious B.C. and Alaska border. But with the threat of American armed intervention in the boundary dispute then occurring, the GTP opted for a more southerly terminus, namely Prince Rupert.

Construction on the route to the west began in Fort William, ON, in 1905 and finally rolled into Prince Rupert in 1914. The GTP met the mountains east of Jasper, and from there to Prince Rupert lay a distance of 850 kilometres (611 miles), with stations every sixteen kilometres. Virtually all of these rural stations were built following the usual single-storey pattern, with a small dormer in the gable above the operators' bay. Of the hundreds of such structures, only three are known to survive today (Dunster, Kwinitsa at Prince Rupert, and Penny at Prince George). The route was much less challenging than that overcome by either the CPR or the Canadian Northern Railway. The mountain passes and river crossings were less formidable than those farther south, although the route does contain its share of high trestles, long bridges, and tunnels. VIA Rail's scenic train, the *Skeena*, follows this historic route, while the *Rocky Mountaineer* shares that portion of the line from Prince George east to Jasper. A roadside plaque beside Highway 16 at Fort Fraser, 137 kilometres west of Prince George marks the driving of the last spike there in April of 1914.

The Canadian Northern Railway (CNoR)

This is the railway of which legends are made. It was the product of the entrepreneurial spirit of William McKenzie and Donald Mann, former CPR contractors, who started with a short line in Manitoba and built it into a cross-country empire from Yarmouth, Nova Scotia, to Vancouver, B.C. Like the GTP, their railway entered the mountains at Jasper through the Yellowhead Pass, but instead of continuing directly west, it followed instead the valley of the North Thompson River, travelling south between the mighty mountain ranges, passing the Premier Range and Mount Robson and Mount Terry Fox. It joined the South Thompson at Kamloops, and west of that followed the steep canyon of the Fraser River southwest to Vancouver. The line was completed in January of 1915 and the last spike driven at Basque, B.C., near Ashcroft, where a roadside plaque marks the event.

In total, the railway ran over eight hundred kilometres (550 miles) on its journey from Jasper to Vancouver. While it needed to surmount no lofty passes, the steep valley of the Thompson required tunnels and high bridges. The route down the Fraser Valley was not an easy one either. While blasting a right of way for the railway near the foaming Hells Gate rapids on the Fraser, the construction workers caused an avalanche that nearly blocked the river completely — something that almost completely destroyed the salmon runs and which took several years to remedy.

Today, most of the original remains of the railway are gone. There do remain, however, a few examples of its classic stations. The CNoR used a somewhat greater variety of station patterns than did the GTP, although the most common was the one with the iconic, two-storey, pyramid-roof style. Most of these examples are gone, of course, with examples still surviving at Fort Langley (museum), and Boston Bar (proposed museum).

The Pacific Great Eastern Railway (PGE)

This line began as the Howe Sound, Pemberton Valley and Northern Railway, chartered in 1912 to run from the deep-water port of Squamish to Prince George in the B.C. interior. From Squamish, the line inched inland over the Coast Range through the daunting Cheakamus Canyon before meeting the Fraser River at the gold-rush town of Lillooet. By 1921, it had reached Quesnel, some 560 kilometres from Squamish, where it halted until the railway figured out a way to finance the perilous construction through the Cottonwood Canyon.

A short section of track was laid from Squamish to North Vancouver in 1914, but it was closed after just fourteen years, while a few tracks were laid south from Prince George, which basically went nowhere until the Cottonwood Canyon could be conquered. Despite its being incomplete, the stunning mountain and lakeside scenery attracted tourists and gamesmen alike and a string of resorts and lodges appeared along the way.

By 1956, the rails were finally pushed through the Cottonwood Canyon, reaching Prince George (and beyond). The link into North Vancouver was re-established, where the route followed the cliff-lined Pacific shore. In 1972, the B.C. government assumed the line, calling it BC Rail and began to run popular scenic and dinner excursions, especially those behind the iconic Royal Hudson steam locomotive. However, in a short-sighted effort to curtail high costs, BC Rail ended its steam excursion in 2001 and passenger service altogether in 2002. Then, in 2003, CN Rail took over the line's operations. Despite the end of a popular day trip from North Vancouver to Whistler, the *Rocky Mountaineer* instituted a scenic run from North Vancouver to Prince George and Jasper. A daily shuttle, known as the *Kaoham Shuttle*, follows a portion of the BC Rail route along the scenic shores of Seton Lake between Lillooet and Seton Portage. Although serving primarily the local First Nations communities, the shuttle has become a popular tourist draw.

Most of the PGE's structures and early stations are gone; the two-storey stations at Quesnel and Williams Lake are the only surviving examples of early PGE station buildings.

The American Invaders

The main reason for the CPR's southern route was to cut off the invasion of U.S. rail lines, whose owners were anxious to creep across the border and reap the mineral bounties of southern British Columbia and southwestern Alberta. Here lay deposits of silver, copper, gold, zinc, and especially coal, which attracted the attention of James J. Hill and his Great Northern Railway.

Hill had been part of the original CPR consortium, but after a falling out with the CPR's Van Horne, he turned his attention to building a rival railroad, the Great Northern. It was formed in 1889 and a year later had tracks crossing the border into the Kootenay and Crowsnest areas, and along the Pacific Coast into New Westminster. He handily beat the CPR into the Kootenay region and by 1893 had managed to lay tracks from Spokane, Washington, right up to the outskirts of Nelson, where the CPR's charter with the Columbia and Kootenay Railway forced it to terminate. The GNR later made its way into Nelson by way of Troup Junction — for some reason now lost in time, the latter was nicknamed Bogustown — and then by running rights on the CPR itself.

By 1902, Hill had constructed track to Elko in the Crowsnest coal fields, and to Yahk by 1907. By 1911, the GNR had opened a line through Princeton to Brookmere, over part of which it shared running rights with the CPR's KVR. During the 1930s and '40s, however, most of the GNR's trackage was abandoned. The only early American lines to have survived are those into Nelson and Yahk, where they link with what is left of the CPR's southern route, and are now part of the massive Burlington Northern empire.

Farther to the west, the GNR built a route along the Pacific Coast from Seattle into Vancouver, where it erected a large classical station adjacent to that built by the Canadian Northern Railway. The GNR station was demolished in 1965, ostensibly to avoid paying municipal taxes, and moved into the CN station. The coastal rail line still exists and remains busy with freight traffic, with Amtrak's route to Portland and with a route run by the *Rocky Mountaineer*.

British Columbia Electric Railway Company (BCER)

Formed from three separate electric railways that had been built previously, the BCER came into being when those three were amalgamated in 1897. With terminals in downtown Vancouver and New Westminster, routes extended to Chilliwack and Fraser Mills. These routes were travelled by handsome interurban cars, which could also carry some freight. Between 1944 and 1958, however, the passenger routes were gradually eliminated, with the passengers being relegated to buses.

In 1989, the B.C. government sold portions of the line to the Southern Railway of British Columbia, which operates a freight service on the route to this day. Other portions became part of Vancouver's popular SkyTrain service, while still others now lie beneath the Trans-Canada Highway. Scant evidence remains of this once vital service. An attempt to operate one of the historic trams as a tourist attraction began in 1998, but it ran into financial constraints and a lack of political interest and after 2011 ended its operation. Only two of the interurban cars remain on display: #1223 in the Burnaby Village Museum; and #1235 in Ottawa's Museum of Science and Technology. The solid terminal buildings, on the other hand, still survive in both New Westminster and downtown Vancouver, while the tiny Vorce tram station shelter stands beside the car barn in the Burnaby Village Museum.

CONQUERING THE MOUNTAINS: THE TUNNELS AND BRIDGES

THE CHALLENGE

Take a piece of aluminum foil and push it together. Note the series of ridges. Now imagine each ridge being thousands of metres high. Take a piece of string and wind it through the ridges keeping it is level as possible. That was the challenge that confronted the railway men as they approached the mountains of western Canada. Not only did they need to wind tracks through the ridges, but they also needed to cross over the gaps and tunnel beneath the summits. Nowhere else in Canada, or, indeed, North America, did the railway builders achieve such astonishing feats of engineering as with the bridges and the tunnels of the West. In fact, western Canada could, and still can, boast that it has more bridges and tunnels per mile or kilometre of track than anywhere else on the continent — and those bridges are among the highest and tunnels the longest.

The grades of these mountains presented a major challenge, as many of the passes were steep, with little room on their often vertical slopes to blast out a right

of way. The major passes included the Kicking Horse through the Rocky Mountains, at 1,800 metres (5,340 feet) above sea level; the Rogers Pass through the Selkirk Mountains, at 1,250 metres (3,779 feet) above sea level; the Eagle Pass through the Monashee Mountains, at an elevation of 600 metres (1,801 feet); and Notch Hill over the Shuswap Highlands at 500 metres (1,692 feet). The initial construction encountered grades of 4.5 percent (i.e., a rise of 4.5 feet per 100 feet of track) most notably on the "Big Hill" in the Kicking Horse Pass at Field. The maximum allowable grade was more like 2.2 percent. This obstacle was overcome in 1909 with the opening of the Spiral Tunnels.

Those who travel by train or car through the mountains of western Alberta and British Columbia can only marvel at the gaping canyons. The railway builders gaped too, but for a different reason. They were overwhelmed by the sight and more than a little perplexed regarding how they were going to be able to build through the Rogers Pass near Field, the lower Kicking Horse Canyon near Golden, the Illecillewaet

The Rocky Mountaineer *crosses the Lillooet bridge in the Fraser Canyon, one of many similar bridges built to conquer the mighty canyon. (Courtesy of* Rocky Mountaineer.*)*

Canyon near Revelstoke, the Thompson Canyon near Lytton, and the Fraser Canyon near Yale, not to mention the incredible Myra Canyon and the Coquihalla Canyons on the KVR.

Nearly everywhere, the first bridges were wooden trestles. Timber was plentiful and the railway men were in a hurry to lay the track and get the trains running. But few lasted. Wood burns, and the forest fires endemic to the forests of the West took their toll. Wood also rots. As trains grew longer and heavier, the bridges needed to become stronger. As a result, the early wooden trestles were soon replaced with those of steel, or, where the chasms were shallow or narrow enough, they were simply filled in.

Frame trestles were the first to appear. They were constructed of wooden frames about every fourteen feet, with the timber being about one-foot square and sixteen-feet long. Pile trestles were those built upon wooden pilings, with the rails laid on wooden decks over the top. Stone-arch spans were usually for shorter and shallower crossings, and as the name implies were stone archways. The West exhibited few of these. Girder spans were a criss-cross construction of steel beams upon which the tracks were laid. Truss spans had the steel frames above the tracks and could appear as arches or straight. Cantilever bridges were supported from the ends of the bridges by means of angled beams.

The Bridges of the Rogers Pass

One of the few feasible passages through the Selkirk Mountains is the Rogers Pass. However, it is a steep and tortuous route of many mountain barriers and yawning canyons. When the railway was being pushed through there, avalanches and fifty-foot snow drifts slowed construction to a crawl. The first bridges were trestles, constructed of log, but as these were prone to fire and weathering, they were soon replaced with those of steel. As trains became longer and heavier, many of the steeper portions of track were levelled and straightened, but this meant more tunnels, and today many of North America's most stunning engineering feats are those the CPR's construction crews put in place.

The Stoney Creek Bridge

Of the many railway bridges constructed across the yawning chasms that can be found in Canada's western mountains, perhaps the most photographed is that over Stoney Creek. Located eleven kilometres north of Glacier

The Loop Creek trestle was abandoned early on as the CPR straightened its route through the Rogers Pass.

and a short distance west of the Trans-Canada Highway, it consists of a steel arch nearly 180 metres (520 feet) long and a dizzying 108 metres (325 feet) above the creek below. One of the CPR's highest bridges in the country, it was completed in 1893, although the first crossing was made in 1884 using a wooden bridge. The arches were doubled in 1929 to accommodate the heavier trains.

Only four kilometres away is the Surprise Creek Bridge. Roughly 138 metres, or 416 feet long, it consists of three truss spans and earned its name because the trains come upon it so suddenly.

The Loop Trail Bridge Ruins

Rogers Pass National Historic Site offers day hikes to many of the park's railway heritage sites. The Loop Brook Trail is a 1.6-kilometre path, steep in sections, to the stone piers of the CPR's original bridge across Loop Creek. The trail leads to the top of one of the piers to provide an overview of the remaining piers. The bridge was built in 1908, replacing the original wooden trestle. The bridge did not last and was abandoned in 1916 in favour of the Spiral Tunnels.

Other trails lead to the site of the famous Glacier House, while the solid form of the CPR's abandoned stone-arch bridges over Cascade Creek and the Illecillewaet River lie along hiking trails close to the Trans-Canada Highway. Although neither is long or high, the CPR's stone-arch bridges are noteworthy, as masonry bridges are rare in western Canada. Now abandoned, they lie on a trail in the Rogers Pass Park. The 1885 Rails Trail follows 3.8 kilometres of the original line of the CPR that connects Loop Brook Campground and Illecillewaet Campground. Because it is on an old railway grade, the walking is very easy. Interpretive signs along the route will relive the exciting history of the railway through Rogers Pass, and describe the location and deadly challenges of the original Rogers Pass Station and townsite.

Revelstoke

Eventually the tracks ease down from the mountains to the large and busy divisional town of Revelstoke, with its yards, newer station, and popular railway museum. But it also contains one of the longer bridges on the CPR main line and that is the 330-metre (1,100-foot) span across the Columbia River in the town itself. The current bridge has had three predecessors, one built in 1885, the second in 1907, and the third in 1968. With its four spans of fifty metres or 150 feet each and seven of twenty-five metres (seventy-five feet), it uses the longest welded-steel-girder spans in North America. Farther west, another significant bridge crosses the Sicamous Narrows with five plate-girder spans and a swing span stretching 148 metres (383 feet).

Over the Thompson

It is at the junction of the North Thompson and South Thompson Rivers that the main-line tracks of the CN and CP finally encounter each other. The latter have been in place since the building of the national dream in 1884 while the former are more recent, dating from the time that the Canadian Northern Pacific Railway laid them in 1914 and 1915, as the railway made its way down the North Thompson. While the CP tracks keep to the south bank and the CN to north, a branch of the CN does cross from Kamloops Junction into downtown Kamloops over the South Thompson, part of a now-abandoned CN branch that formerly, in partnership with a CP branch, led to Kelowna and allowed the CN access to downtown Kamloops. Here the CN erected a grand brick station that still stands.

The CNR bridge over the North Thompson River at Kamloops is one of the longest in the region.

South Thompson Bridge

One of the two CN bridges that cross the South Thompson, giving access to the downtown station (used now only by the Kamloops Steam Railway tour train), is a curving steel-deck truss bridge measuring over three hundred metres (nine hundred feet) with five deck-plate girders and four through-plate girders. One sixty-five-metre (208-foot) through-truss swing span was incorporated into the structure in 1927 to

allow, by law, possible river traffic along the Thompson, which by then was nearly non-existent.

North Thompson Bridge

The CN's current main-line bridge over the North Thompson River extends nearly 380 metres (1,138 feet) with fifteen deck-plate girder spans and a swing span, which has remained fixed in position since 1937. The bridge itself dates to 1915 with the construction of the

Canadian Northern Railway. Before encountering the canyon of the Fraser River at Lytton, the CN crosses the Thompson River no fewer than seven more times. Three of the structures are quite massive. At forty-six kilometres from Kamloops, the tracks cross the river on a 260-metre-long, twenty-five-metre-high bridge, built from one through-truss span and six through-plate girder spans. That which lies just nine kilometres farther on, near the ghost settlement of Walhachin, measures 380 metres and rises eighteen metres above the river using deck-plate girders, while the third crosses on twelve deck-plate girders eighteen metres above the river.

The Cisco Bridges

At Ashcroft, the Thompson River bends sharply southward, travelling some distance before emptying into the muddy waters of the Fraser River at Lytton. From here, the Fraser Canyon steepens dramatically as it makes its way southward. For almost the entire length of the Fraser River canyon, the CP and CN cling to opposite sides of the gorge on the often precarious slopes of the canyon walls. The perilous nature of the canyon is reflected in names of rapids like the Jaws of Death Gorge and Hells Gate.

On their respective journeys along the banks of the turbulent Fraser River, which guided both rail lines through the mountains, the CN and CP stuck to their own sides of the riverbed. But at Cisco which was originally known as Siska, near Lytton, they cross the river and each other. The older of the two lines, the CPR, erected its first bridge across the canyon in 1883, replacing it with a newer span in 1910. The original cantilever span rested on stone piers placed well above the

high water mark of the tumultuous waters. The current structure is the shorter of the two bridges; its three truss spans (two Pratt trusses and one Parker truss) extend 160 metres in total. Upon reaching the west bank, the rails plunge directly into the Cantilever Bar Tunnel. The original cantilever bridge was dismantled and placed over the Niagara Canyon on the CPR's E&N line on Vancouver Island.

The CNR bridge, built by the Canadian Northern Railway in 1915, is a 247-metre truss-arch bridge looming ninety metres above the brown waters of the river. The bridges are about one hundred metres apart. The Cisco Siding Road on the Trans-Canada Highway south of Lytton leads to a vantage point over the canyon and a distant view of this unusual bridge crossing.

Bridges of the Lower Mainland
The Harrison River Bridge

As the CPR swings out of the tumultuous Fraser Canyon and into the lush farmlands of the Fraser River delta it encounters two long bridges. That over the Harrison River stretches over 315 metres (950 feet) and rests on eleven piers, including, because the Harrison River is deemed "navigable," a swing span.

The Pitt River Bridge

About sixty-five kilometres farther along, as the line approaches Coquitlam, it crosses the Pitt River Bridge. Over 575 metres (1,750 feet) long, it consists of four through-truss spans and nine deck-plate girder spans as well as an interlocking swing span.

Fraser River CPR Bridge

Listed on the Mission Historical Society inventory of historic places, the CPR bridge over the Fraser River is one of the Lower Mainland's longest, and connects U.S. rail lines with the CPR lines in British Columbia. At nearly six hundred metres or 1,700 feet long, it connects Matsqui in the south with Mission in the north. When it opened in 1891, it was the only rail link to the United States. Originally built of wood, it was only the second bridge over that river, and operated with a swing span to allow the sternwheelers to glide through the opening. It was the first of the nine spans to be converted to steel, in 1903; the remaining spans were converted over the next decade.

There was no road connection over the river, however, and vehicles had to resort to a long ferry crossing. Finally, in 1927, the B.C. government laid planks across the bridge to allow vehicles to cross. Even then, though, it was still only a single lane in each direction. The bridge was damaged in 1955 when one of the trusses fell into the river, causing the motor traffic to once again revert to ferry crossings. Eventually, in 1973 a new road bridge opened, and the CPR bridge once again reverted to rail traffic only.

The modern Fraser River CPR Bridge is made up of eight fifty-metre, through-truss steel girders, which rest upon a dozen concrete piers. The swing span, which measures seventy-eight metres (230 feet) rests on its own separate piers. Good views of the bridge are from the Captain's Cabin Neighbourhood Pub on Abbott St., or from the Highway 11 bridge.

Bridges of the Grand Trunk Pacific

The GTP, routing as it did through the Skeena River Valley, encountered fewer daunting challenges than did the CPR farther south.

The Old Skeena Bridge

Built by the Grand Trunk Pacific Railway and opened to the public in 1925 as a combined automobile-railway bridge meant to replace a ferry service, the "old Skeena Bridge" crosses the Skeena River between the City of Terrace and the community of Thornhill. The curving bridge, which includes two through trusses and three deck trusses, curves across the river, stretching more than three hundred metres. In 1953, with the laying of tracks on a new branch line from Terrace to Kitimat, the CNR undertook major renovations to the railway section of the bridge, while road improvements in 2001 included replacing the plank deck with steel. Meanwhile a re-routing of Highway 16 over Ferry Island has lessened the load on the old road bridge. The bridge was listed on the Canadian Register of Historic Places in 2005.

Prince George Fraser River Bridge

As the GTP pressed westward, it encountered the wide waters of the Fraser River. Here, in 1914, the railway erected an 815-metre bridge consisting of a main vertical-lift span and twelve approach spans. Although the lift span is one of the shortest, it is this portion that makes the bridge one of the more unusual railway bridges on the continent. Designed by bridge engineer Joseph Strauss, and built by the Canadian Bridge Company of Walkerville, Ontario, it had just three counterparts in the United States, only one of which remains, and it is likely the only surviving example in Canada. It is considered nationally significant. Instead of using towers and cables to lift the span, this design incorporates counterweights attached to the approach spans. The lift span has remained fixed for many years. The town marked the one-hundredth anniversary of the bridge on January 27, 2014.

––––––

Other crossings of the Skeena include that over Seeley Gulch, rising sixty metres above the valley floor and extending 275 metres across it. At Gitsegukla, the tracks cross a 288-metre bridge fifty metres above the Skeena River.

The Legends of the Kettle Valley Railway

Of all the heritage rail routes in British Columbia, the story of the iconic Kettle Valley Railway is the most legendary, and loved. By the time it was finished in 1916, after six years of construction through some of southern British Columbia's most challenging terrain, it linked the southern route of the CPR from Midway with the CPR main line at Hope and Spences Bridge. This gave the railway its cherished southern link to the coast. While the mountain barriers and the dizzying defiles were less daunting than those on the original main line, those who hike or bike the rail trail will testify that the bridges and the tunnels represent some of the CPR's greatest feats of engineering.

The Trout Creek Trestle, Summerland, B.C.

Completed in 1912, the Trout Creek Trestle is the highest on the KVR. At more than seventy-three metres (235 feet), it provides a dizzying view down the valley, while it spans 188 metres (616 feet). The trestle has been described as the third highest steel girder of its type in North America. It now forms one of the most thrilling sections of the Kettle Valley Rail Trail and of the Kettle Valley Steam Railway excursions. While the most exhilarating way to view the bridge is to actually cross, those hesitant to appreciate the vertigo-inducing drop may take in the gorge and trestle from the south side of the gorge by following the Kettle Valley Rail Trail in Summerland.

Bridal Veil Falls

The last of the KVR's timber trestles to be built was that over the Bridal Veil Falls east of Hope. Its thirty-two-metre (106-foot) wooden truss span rested atop forty-metre-high (120-foot) wooden towers. Today, those historic timbers rest in a heap at the bottom of the valley. Access to the site is via the Coquihalla River Trail east of Hope.

Myra Canyon's Trestles — McCulloch's Wonder: Part 1

While the Okanagan Highlands may not appear as intimidating as the mighty mountain chains farther east, they nonetheless posed a major challenge to McCulloch, the KVR's engineer. The Myra Canyon was particularly daunting. Carved by the KVO and Pooley Creeks, the canyon looms nearly one thousand metres above the Okanagan Valley and takes the form of a wide bowl.

Another of McCulloch's marvels were the string of trestles carved into the Myra Canyon walls high above Kelowna.

To conquer the chasm, the KVR carved its right of way into the near vertical slope more than nine hundred metres above Kelowna. Thanks to the many creeks and side canyons that carve up the canyon wall, the railway needed eighteen trestles, all clinging to the nearly vertical canyon slopes, and two tunnels to navigate that route. They were almost immediately recognized as a major feat of railway engineering and nicknamed "McCulloch's Wonder."

Following the closure of the line in 1972, the historic trestles fell into disrepair. Two decades later, the Myra Canyon Trestle Restoration Society went to work and restored the route and its trestles for a hiking and cycling trail. It quickly became one of the world's most popular trails, and in 2003, the B.C. government designated the canyon as a provincial park.

But the hot and dry weather in British Columbia's interior, (the Okanagan is Canada's hottest and driest region) has led to many devastating fires there, none more devastating than that which occurred in August of 2003. Flames raced through twenty-thousand acres of tinder-dry woodland, consuming two hundred homes in Kelowna and twelve of the eighteen trestles along the canyon wall. Due to the high heritage value of the canyon's trestles, all levels of government, along with private donors, coordinated funds to begin restoration. Although fire once again destroyed Trestle #3 in 2013, the trail now offers scenic if dizzying cycling and walking opportunities.

The various trestles, which differ in height and length, all offer captivating sights, but none offer sights as spectacular as those from the trestle that crosses Pooley Creek — the largest and highest of these structures (and the most daunting), it soars 55 metres above the creek and stretches 225 metres. It is at this point that many novice cyclists stop and turn around. The other trestles may range from 27 metres to 130 metres, but none are as high as that which crosses Pooley Creek.

Access to the trail is via the Myra Canyon Forest Service Road, an eight-and-one-half-kilometre gravel road that leads to a parking lot and trail access. To reach it, follow McCulloch Road southeast of the City of Kelowna.

The Similkameen Trestles

It seems that the Myra Canyon was not McCulloch's only engineering conquest. The Copper Mountain Branch of the KVR, which ran from Princeton to the mines at Copper Mountain south of Princeton, contained no fewer than thirty wooden trestles within a fourteen-kilometre section, fifteen within a mere four kilometres. Meanwhile, four tunnels were blasted out within a little over a kilometre. McCulloch finished the line in 1920, but the vagaries

of copper prices made the line an on-again-off-again operation. Finally, in 1957 the mine closed for good and the line was torn up. While a rail trail follows some of the old road bed, the remainder has fallen victim to new developments, or has deteriorated to the point where only the ruins of the trestles remain.

The Railway Bridges of Vancouver

Vancouver was a railway town from the get-go. It became the western terminus for the CPR in 1886 and, surrounded by a number of watery channels, it is inevitable that it acquired a large number of railway bridges, many of them lengthy and subject to the challenges of ocean freight traffic.

The Fraser River Swing Bridge

This important structure was built in 1904 and links Vancouver with both eastern Canada and the United States. It crosses the Fraser River in New Westminster. To accommodate this junction, a special "spread span" was constructed at the east end, wider than the others and forming a "Y" to allow the tracks to diverge, giving it an unusual appearance. In its original form, it contained two levels, one for trains and the other for vehicles. But when the Pattullo Bridge opened to vehicles in 1937, the vehicle deck on the rail bridge was removed. Originally built with a 125-metre swing span, which had to be moved into place at low tide to allow the four barges to safely work beneath it, its overall length is 542 metres and consists of seven approach spans plus the main swing span. A collision with a boat in 1976 required extensive repairs to one of the fixed spans.

The Second Narrows Railway Bridge

The best known of the city's bridge names is the Second Narrows Bridge over the Burrard Inlet east of downtown Vancouver — not the railway bridge, but rather the highway bridge. This dates to the tragic collapse of the Second Narrows Highway Bridge, which, while under construction, collapsed in June 17, 1958, taking the lives of seventy-nine workers. In 1994, a memorial to the dead workers was unveiled and is known as the Ironworkers Memorial.

The notion of a rail bridge over the Second Narrows dates to the anticipation around the Yukon gold rush. As early as the 1890s, the Pacific Great Eastern and the Canadian Northern railways had planned to cross the inlet with a rail line leading to the Yukon. But with the bankruptcy of the CNoR in 1918, those plans never gelled. Although the railway builders chomped at the bit to lay tracks to the north shore of the Burrard Inlet and much needed extra dock space, it was not until 1925 that the CNR erected a combined car-rail bridge to link the two shores.

The bridge consisted of several spans, one of which was a forty-six-metre bascule-lift span to allow ship traffic to pass beneath. But the span proved too great a lure for the many vessels that struck it frequently. Exasperated, the CNR sold the bridge to the B.C. government which replaced the bascule span with a vertical-lift span. But the crashes continued to plague the unfortunate bridge. Eventually, in 1970 the entire structure was replaced with a new bridge and larger lift span. Trains crossing the new bridge, upon reaching the south shore, immediately enter the 3.4-kilometre Thornton Tunnel which takes them to the main line in Willingdon.

The Bridges of Vancouver Island
Kinsol Trestle

Although the CNR hasn't run a train on Vancouver Island since 1980, its former route offers one of the nation's largest wooden trestles, the Kinsol Trestle north of Shawnigan Lake. Built in 1920 by the Canadian Northern Pacific Railway after its 1918 merger with the CNR, the trestle stands forty-four metres high, measures 188 metres long, and has an unusual seven-degree curve. But wooden bridges don't last, and soon after the line was abandoned the Kinsol Trestle fell into disrepair. It took $5.7 million from the Cowichan Valley Regional District to restore the bridge to accommodate hikers and cyclists. It reopened to trail users in 2011. Today the bridge is considered to be the tallest and longest-surviving free-standing wooden trestle in the world.

Visitors can find parking on the south side of the trestle not far from the Trans-Canada Highway. Exit onto Shawnigan Lake Road, turn left onto Renfrew Road and then right onto Glen Eagles Road, then follow the signs to the "Historic Kinsol Trestle" parking lot. For those reluctant to defy the dizzying height, an interpretive trail leads down to the creek below. The bridge lies on the Cowichan Valley Rail Trail, where three more bridges have been prepared for hikers and cyclists. These include those at Holt Creek, Marie Canyon, and McGee Creek.

Todd Creek Trestle

Another one of the last wooden trestles on western Canada's rail lines is that over Todd Creek. It is a curving structure, which rises above the narrow, wooded gorge of Todd Creek. From 1911 to 1980 the bridge carried lengthy CN logging trains transporting Douglas fir timber from Sooke to Victoria. Part of the Galloping Goose Rail Trail between Victoria and Sooke, it has been planked in for easy hiking and cycling. The trail continues to reveal examples of old growth Douglas fir along the route. A walking trail that leads to the Todd Creek offers a stunning vantage point from which to see the engineering feat from below.

Niagara Creek Bridge

Canada it seems has more than one Niagara Gorge. The less famous of the two is that on Vancouver Island. When the Esquimalt and Nanaimo Railway was under construction in 1886, it needed to cross the deep gorge of Niagara Creek. To replace the original wooden bridge, built in 1885 using 400,000 board feet of lumber, the CPR disassembled its steel cantilever bridge from Cisco on its main line near Lytton in the Fraser Canyon, and in 1911 reconstructed it a few dozen metres from the original Niagara bridge, over the gorge. The twenty-one-panel Pratt-truss deck measures 160 metres, with the main span measuring ninety-six metres while soaring eighty metres above the creek. The spans rest on two stone piers set deep in the Malahat Mountains, nine kilometres from Victoria. The bridge carried the route of VIA Rail's *Malahat* passenger train over the canyon until service was suspended in 2011. At this writing, there continues to be ongoing discussion as to the possible revision of that service or at least a portion of it.

Arbutus Canyon Trestle

This curving steel trestle on the E&N line is 141 metres long and sixty-seven metres high, and is equally as impressive as the Niagara Creek Bridge, which sits a short distance away. It consists of a series of Pratt trusses. During the suspension of train service along the line, various so-called daredevils have ventured across the open ties on foot, some even on motorcycles, posting their feats on YouTube.

Under the Mountains: the Tunnels
The Spiral Tunnels

Of Canada's many historic railway tunnels, perhaps the best known are the legendary Spiral Tunnels of the Kicking Horse Pass. Of the many options to conquer the steep Rocky Mountains grades, the Kicking Horse was the ultimate choice. Known as the Big Hill, the 4.5 percent grade was exceptionally steep, especially for the locomotives of the day, and required the addition of extra locomotives to help the trains up the hill. Downhill was a problem too, as the first train to attempt it derailed, killing three crew.

But one of the railway's design engineers came up with a solution, The Spiral Tunnels. And in 1909 they finally replaced the Big Hill. After leaving the former divisional town of Field, the tracks cross the Kicking Horse River and enter the tunnel under Mt. Ogden. They then spiral to the left inside the tunnel for 890 metres and emerge fifteen metres higher. Crossing the river once more, the trains then enter Cathedral Mountain, this time spiralling to the right and emerging at the top of the Pass seventeen metres higher than when they entered.

A viewpoint and interpretation centre lies beside the Trans-Canada Highway 7.4 kilometres east of Field and another along the Yoho Valley Road 2.3 kilometres

The Spiral Tunnels remain an engineering marvel to this day.

from the Trans-Canada Highway. Tourists may well be rewarded with a passing train as up to thirty lengthy CPR freights may pass each day. Yoho National Park also maintains the Walk in the Past Trail — a 1.2-kilometre path that leads to one of the early abandoned spurs and an old locomotive used in the tunnels' construction. The TCH actually follows the roadbed of the original CPR track alignment.

The Connaught and Mount Macdonald Tunnels

After the conquest of the Kicking Horse Pass, the railway men had to face another test: Rogers Pass and another mountain range, this time the Selkirks, to be burrowed through. After the line opened in 1886, avalanches proved to be a problem. One, in 1899, destroyed the Rogers Pass station, killing seven. Then, when another, in 1910, just 1.6 kilometres from the earlier slide, killed sixty-two work crew clearing an earlier slide, the CPR decided it was time for a tunnel. In 1916, at a cost of $60 million, the 8.5-kilometre Connaught Tunnel opened. It was the continent's longest tunnel at the time.

It succeeded in avoiding some the worst avalanche routes in the area and eliminated an aggregated 2,300° in track curvature. Along the abandoned track was a scenic winding route that lead to the popular Glacier House resort hotel, which closed a dozen years later.

But when the tunnel became a bottleneck, and required pusher engines for the uphill grade, the CPR undertook yet another tunnel. The Mount Macdonald Tunnel was burrowed ninety metres beneath the Connaught Tunnel. Completed in 1988, the 14.7-kilometre Mount Macdonald Tunnel, costing $500 million, succeeded the Connaught in becoming North America's longest. Today, trains travel eastbound through the Mount Macdonald Tunnel and west through the Connaught Tunnel. To keep the tunnel ventilated, four huge fans force the fumes up an 8.5-metre shaft 350 metres to the surface of Cheops Mountain. The engineering feat was completed in 1988 and is listed as an inductee in the web-based Canadian Railway Hall of Fame.

But it wasn't only the mountains which required extensive tunnelling. As the CPR made its way along the Thompson River west from Kamloops, five tunnels were excavated into the Cherry Creek bluffs within less than two kilometres of each other, varying in length from sixty-eight metres (206 feet) to over 212 metres (636 feet). As these are active rails, there is no tourism access. Farther downstream, about eight kilometres south of Ashcroft, the CN enters a pair of long tunnels, the Cornwall Creek Tunnel at three hundred metres and the Black Canyon Tunnel at more than four hundred metres long. Across the river, the CPR makes its way through a tunnel more than 150 metres long.

The Quintette Tunnels — McCulloch's Wonder: Part 2

Andrew McCulloch was in the habit of creating railway engineering marvels. The need to conquer three major mountain ranges resulted in the world's most expensive railway line of the day at over $300,000 per mile. Part of that reason was the Coquihalla River Gorge. His Kettle Valley Railway did not follow a particularly easy route and needed some engineering ingenuity. The Myra Canyon Trestles exemplify this. But those uncomfortable with the dizzying heights of the trestles will find the Quintette Tunnels near Hope equally astounding, but easier on the nerves.

Here the river has carved a twisting gorge more than one hundred metres deep and through the world's hardest rock. Cliff ladders, hanging baskets, and suspension bridges were all needed to survey the route. The blasting and bridging was finally finished in 1916, resulting in four tunnels and short trestles. McCulloch named the tunnels after one of his favourite Shakespearean plays, *Othello*.

Now preserved in a provincial park, the trail through the tunnels has become popular with hikers and cyclists, and families in search of a day's outing. The site offers a shady parking lot with picnic tables and interpretive plaques. Four tunnels through the dank granite walls lead to short footbridges, built into the railway trestles over the foaming waters, which plunge between the deep narrow gorges there.

The Quintette Tunnels near Hope were considered to be one of McCulloch's marvels when he built the ill-fated Kettle Valley Railway.

Note the wooden support in Tunnel 1 and the decorative concrete entrances to Tunnel 2. The stunning canyon and tunnels have caught the eye of the Hollywood movie makers, who have shot portions of *Rambo, (First Blood)*, starring Sylvester Stallone, *Far From Home,* with Matt Frewer and Drew Barrymore, and *Shoot to Kill,* which starred Sidney Poitier, in the spectacular canyon. Access to the canyon is from Highway 5, a short distance north of Hope.

The Clapperton Tunnel

It may not be large or complicated, but the Clapperton Tunnel is the only tunnel along the KVR to boast stone-arch portals. This 110-metre long tunnel lies beside Highway 8 about sixteen kilometres south of Spences Bridge.

THE FACES OF THE RAILWAYS: THE HERITAGE RAILWAY STATIONS

Unlike on the Prairies and in eastern Canada, in the mountain ranges of western Alberta and British Columbia the railways had little choice regarding where they could route their lines and locate their stations. Lines across Manitoba, Saskatchewan, and eastern and central Alberta were for the most part relatively straight, with stations and grid-like towns and villages appearing at intervals of roughly fifteen kilometres. In fact, the railways laid out and named most of those towns themselves.

This was much the same in southern Ontario and Quebec, as well as in much of the Maritimes. But in the mountainous regions of southwestern Alberta and in most of British Columbia, the mountain passes and the river valleys dictated the routes of the rails. Except in the flat valley lands, there was little opportunity or reason for towns to develop, with the important exception of the divisional towns, and even these offered little more than the basic requirements of the railways such as maintenance facilities and facilities for the railway employees.

For the most part, the stations repeated the railways' standard patterns. Neither the Canadian Northern nor the Grand Trunk Pacific railways varied often from the three or four simple patterns that they repeated across much of the country. The CPR stuck pretty much to its pattern book as well, although CP did use a greater variety of patterns.

Stations typically filled a variety of roles in Canada's communities. Not only was the agent responsible for keeping the trains moving, his role in the community also included collecting the mail, shipping freight, and even soliciting local business. Along with the local preacher and pool hall operator, he was often considered one of the key members of the community. Townspeople would often gather in the station waiting room, not just to collect their mail, or send a telegraph, but also to hear the local news coming in via the telegraph wire, including the vital Stanley Cup hockey scores. Often, too, in the early days, the station had the town's only telephone, and so the agent may have functioned as the town telephone operator.

But the mountains offered opportunities for the railway companies to attract tourists to the skiing, the spas, and the wildlife, and so it was in such locales that more elegant station styles were used — the stations in Banff, Jasper, and Lake Louise are prime surviving examples of the more sophisticated designs the railways adopted for this purpose. These were built along with the grand hotels such as the Chateau Lake Louise, the Banff Springs Hotel, and the Jasper Park Lodge. Happily, in these instances, stations and lodges still survive.

THE STATION BUILDERS

Ralph Benjamin Pratt

Pratt became one of Canada's early railway station architects. Most of his work was for the stations of the Canadian Northern Railway, for which he devised the CNoR's iconic pyramid-roofed depot. The most common form was the block-like, two-storey "second-class" station found at most the CNoR's rural locations. For the larger, divisional locations, he adapted the second-class form by adding an extension to each end, with dormers, either peak gable or hip gable, appearing in the roofline.

Born in London, England, where he trained as an architect, Pratt moved to Winnipeg in 1892, and the following year became an architect for the CPR, for which he designed many of that line's chateau-style buildings. Soon after, the CNoR lured him away. As well as designing their stations, he also devised many other structures as well. He later formed the well-known architectural partnership known as Pratt and Ross. He passed away in 1950.

Edward Maxwell

This Montreal-born architect, a favourite of the CPR, apprenticed under the great American station designer Henry Hobson Richardson in Boston. Moving back to Montreal, Maxwell went to work for a design firm there. In his designs, he combined the Richardsonian style, with its wide arches and rounded features, with the popular Italian Renaissance style then in vogue. In 1902 he formed a partnership with his brother William and together went on to design many of the CPR's grandest chateau-style structures, including Van Horne's own summer home on Ministers Island in New Brunswick.

One of his first assignments with the CPR was the grand western terminus in Vancouver built in 1897. His work and influence appears in many of western Canada's chateau-style stations, such as those in Vernon, B.C. and New Westminster, B.C., both of which are still standing, as well as the popular CPR dining stations in Field, Glacier, and North Bend, which no longer exist.

Bruce Price

Born in 1845, Price interned at the firm of Niemsee and Neilsen in Baltimore before opening his own firm in Wilkes Barre, Pennsylvania. It was there he caught the eye of fellow American William Van Horne, who engaged him with the CPR.

Price brought his chateau-style architecture to the CPR, designing such structures as the Windsor station in Montreal, and the Banff Springs Hotel in Alberta. His style continued to influence station architecture even following his death in 1903.

John Schofield

Schofield migrated from Ireland in the early 1900s and settled in Winnipeg, where he became a draftsman for the Canadian Northern Railway. Following the CNoR's bankruptcy, he moved to Montreal where, in partnership with John Archibald, he designed many of the newly formed CNR's stations and hotels, including the Hotel Vancouver in 1939. His smaller station designs included those in Chilliwack, B.C. and Hope, B.C., the latter of which still stands. He retired in 1948.

THE STATIONS

Canada's three cross-country rail lines, the CPR, the GTP, and the CNoR, were all anxious to get up and running as quickly as possible. This led to a frenzy of station building. As a result, the railway companies created a series of standard, station-building patterns, which could be sent to local contractors. When the construction frenzy was at its peak, identical stations were being erected across the country, often in different locations simultaneously.

Van Horne knew this, and created a simple pattern, which was little more than a two-storey wooden box, with no architectural embellishment. This served as the design for the first CPR station almost everywhere. As financing improved following the depression of 1890, the CPR was able to replace the old "Van Hornes" with more appealing styles. To do this, it published a pattern book for its stations, which included more than twenty station patterns. These ranged from those with simple pyramid-style roofs, which appeared in many western and mountain towns, especially those along the lesser used branch lines and the southern main line. The busy main line saw a greater variety of station styles. Larger population centres also invited more appealing variations, as did tourist destinations.

The mountains on the main line saw a number of log stations built to reflect the wilderness appeal of the region. Examples still stand at Glacier, B.C., and Lake Louise, Alberta. Stations at Jasper (CNR) and Banff (CPR) also display a rusticity meant to appeal to the wilderness adventurer.

Pratt's pyramid roof dominated the townscapes of most of the CNoR's towns and rural locations, although a few variations were created for variety in different locations. Examples remain in Fort Langley and Boston Bar. But it was the GTP that applied a single standard style almost everywhere throughout the mountains and the West, indeed right across the country. This style is typified by storey-and-a-half structures with a bell-cast roof and a dormer tucked into the roofline. Examples survive in Prince Rupert, B.C., (from Kwinitsa), Prince George, B.C. (Penny), and Dunster, B.C. (now a museum).

In the southern mountains, the American lines imported their simpler styles, of which the station in Salmo is a prime example.

Saving the Stations

Few of the stations that once dotted the railway lines now remain. As a result of changing technology and the decline of passenger travel, fewer stations were needed, and because in most places there was little to nothing by way of a local population to save them, mass demolition could be undertaken without much opposition. Beginning in the 1950s, the railways removed more than 90 percent of their station buildings.

At first there was little outrage. Weren't the railways just doing what was in their economic interest? But when the CPR demolished the tudoresque West Toronto station in 1982, the resulting outcry led to the passing, in 1988, of the federal Heritage Railway Stations Protection Act (HRSPA), designed to prevent the railway companies from demolishing stations that the minister of the environment designated as historically significant. Within a decade, more than one hundred stations across the country were declared heritage buildings. That didn't always guarantee their survival, for many simply stood neglected until arson or deterioration took their toll. Most, however, have become museums or private businesses.

This chapter shows which of these represent heritage sites that the railway enthusiast or those who are simply heritage lovers may visit and celebrate this component of the railway heritage of the mountains of the West. In British Columbia and the mountains of Alberta, fifteen stations enjoy designation under the HRSPA, while an additional two dozen have been repurposed as museums or information centres. Several others have become bars, club houses, or simply private homes. Few actually remain in use by the railways.

Agassiz, B.C. (CPR)

Considered to be one of Canada's oldest surviving wooden CPR stations, that from the rural community of Agassiz now serves as the Agassiz-Harrison Museum. Built in 1893, it is the only example of this style that the CPR built in western Canada. A two-storey wooden building, it retains its Tuscan-red paint scheme. Its barn-style gable on the second-floor roof extends the width of the building. In 1986, the Agassiz-Harrison Historical Society

purchased the station from the railway for one dollar. Under the terms of the special sales deal, the society was required to relocate the station. The building was transported from the tracks to the society's grounds in Harrison Hot Springs, and today the museum displays the history of the area and clothing and artifacts of its early days.

Athalmer, B.C. (CPR)

Now housing the Windermere Valley Historical Society museum and archives, the station, relocated to Windermere from Athalmer, is one of the CPR's rare surviving log stations. It was built in 1923 on the Windermere subdivision, which extended from Golden on the CPR main line to Colvalli in the south. (Other surviving log stations include those at Glacier, Lake Louise, and Laggan — the name given to the first wooden station built at Lake Louise). After a train derailment damaged the building in its original location in 1979, the volunteers of the historical society moved it to its present location where it serves as the main building amid a number of other heritage structures that have also been moved to the museum grounds.

Banff, AB (CPR)

The CPR added this station to its roster of tourist stations in 1910 to replace an earlier log station. The main attraction here was the hot springs, which gave rise to the Banff Springs Hotel, now part of the Fairmont chain. The station reflects what was known as the "arts and crafts" style of architecture. The large two-storey building offers two cross gables, which form the second floor. By the time this station was constructed, Banff

The CPR's Banff station has drawn tourists since the 1890s; however, now most arrive by car.

Now set aside to become a museum, the CNoR station at Boston Bar demonstrates that line's standard divisional point style. Once numerous, few remain today.

National Park was becoming a major tourist draw, and the larger station served not just the hotel but the growing village as well. The building, situated almost a kilometre from the town's centre and two kilometres from the hotel, also contains a café and bus depot. Its construction material intentionally reflects the rusticity of the park, with walls built half from rough timber and half from cut-stone and wood-shingle roofing. It was designated under the HRSPA in 1991. Although the station has been fully preserved itself, the only train to call here now is the *Rocky Mountaineer* tour train, VIA Rail having been pulled out in 1990 with the Mulroney cuts to rail passenger service.

Boston Bar, B.C. (CNoR)

This large Canadian Northern station reflects the style which the CNoR used at its divisional points across Canada. The station, what is known as a "Class 2" station, displays the trademark, two-storey, central pyramid roof of architect Ralph Benjamin Pratt, flanked by single-storey extensions at each end. Dating from 1912, it sits vacant, a short distance back from the still-busy rail yards, awaiting re-use as a museum.

Castlegar, B.C. (CPR)

Built in 1907, the current station-museum replaced an identical building built in 1902. The station was originally situated in the wye of the railway lines that the CPR acquired to complete its southern main line through the Crowsnest Pass. The wooden building sports a second-storey mansard roof with six slanted, recessed dormers, reflecting the area's Germanic influence; bay windows are located on two sides to allow the agents to observe rail traffic on both tracks. The building sits a block away from the town's downtown core and was sold in 1989 to become a museum.

The former CPR station in Castlegar, British Columbia, has been relocated a short distance from the rails to become a museum.

Courtenay, B.C. (CPR)

This solid, two-storey wooden station, built in 1914, marks the end of the line for the Esquimalt and Nanaimo Railway — which was run by the CPR — on Vancouver Island. The main portion of the structure is a two-storey cross gable with four windows, providing sleeping quarters for train crews. From either side, a storey-and-a half extension extends from the main structure. The station was designed by R.A. Bainbridge, the CPR's divisional engineer. In its later years, the station was run by VIA Rail, although as of 2015, no rail service was being offered. It was designated a heritage structure under the HRSPA in 1993, and a heritage building by the town in 2002.

Cranbrook, B.C. (CPR)

While the sleek lines of the CPR divisional station in Cranbrook may resemble the flat-roofed international style of station made popular in the post–Second World War period, it is in fact basically the CPR's original 1898 station. That building collapsed in 1905 when an additional storey was being added. It was later completed, and by 1936 it was three full stories high, with a pair of hip-gable dormers flanking a peak-gable dormer on the third storey. Two-storey extensions marked each end of the structure. In 1946, the roof line was completely altered and the interior modernized to give the station its post-war international style.

In 2009, the CPR moved most of its facilities from Cranbrook to Fort Steele Junction, vacating the building. Since that time, the City of Cranbrook has shown an interest in acquiring the building and restoring it to its 1936 appearance. As of 2015, the station remains unaltered. The yards, however, remain full of railway activity, and the area around the old station is known as Cranbrook's Railway District. Along with the station, it houses the Cranbrook Canadian Museum of Rail Travel (see section on Museums), the relocated Elko station, a CPR train set display, a wooden water tower, and a portion of the railway roundhouse.

Duncan, B.C. (CPR)

This two-storey wooden station was built by the Canadian Pacific Railway in 1912 to replace a smaller Esquimalt and Nanaimo Railway station that had been built in 1887 when the line first opened. The station was built in a straightforward style, with little embellishment, although its size indicated that the CPR expected Duncan to grow into an important regional centre. The station served VIA Rail until 2011, when service was suspended due to track issues. Today, the

Until recently, VIA Rail's Malahat train called at the Duncan, British Columbia, station, a heritage-designated station.

Stations like that in Dunster, British Columbia — now a museum — numbered in the thousands when built by the GTP. Now only a handful remain.

building houses the Cowichan Valley Museum and is designated under the HRSPA. Duncan lies halfway between Victoria and Nanaimo.

Dunster, B.C. (Grand Trunk Pacific)

The little station in the tiny community of Dunster, B.C., situated east of McBride, is a rare surviving example of the GTP's most common station style, used in two-thirds of the communities served by the line and known as Plan 100-152. The station consists of an octagonal operator's bay that extends into a dormer on the roof. In order to save this vanishing station style, the community rescued it from CNR's proposed demolition and moved it a few metres from the track to become a museum, restoring its exterior. Although the station no longer shelters train passengers, the community remains a flag stop for VIA's *Skeena* train service between Jasper and Prince Rupert.

Elko, B.C. (CPR)

The CPR reserved a special set of station plans for its Crowsnest Pass buildings. These displayed a steep gable above the main floor, with a steeply pitched eave that extended the roofline over the platform. These were known simply as "CPR Crowsnest Style B." The CPR built these only on their Crowsnest subdivision and situated them at Aldridge, Crowsnest, Elko, Creston, Fernie, Fort Steele, McGillivray, and Rampart. Built in 1898, those at Fort Steele and Fernie were replaced in 1907 and 1912 respectively. The others survived until the late 1960s, except for that at Elko, which remained in use until 1980. In 1987, the Canadian Museum of Rail Travel, located in Cranbrook, purchased it to display on their museum grounds.

Fernie, B.C. (CPR)

Elko was not the only style distinctive to the CPR's Crowsnest Pass route. One of the largest and most

Built at the peak of southern B.C.'s coal boom, the CPR station in Fernie was set back from the tracks to become a gallery and café.

After the Second World War, the CPR adopted a more modern station style, such as that of the now-closed Field, British Columbia, station.

elegant was that built by the CPR in Fernie, in the heart of a coal mining district. Built in 1908, following a devastating fire that destroyed much of the town, the large wooden structure features wide hip roofs atop its second storey, with broad, bell-cast roofs over its two, single-storey wings. Moved a short distance from its original site in 1990 and restored by the Fernie and District Arts Council, it is today known as the Arts Station, housing art displays and a café as well.

Field, B.C. (CPR)

When the CPR blasted its way through the Kicking Horse Pass in 1884, it established Field as a divisional point, adding a dining station known as the Field House. The first station was a small log structure to help attract tourists to this mountain area. Following the Second World War, the railway began to modernize, and replaced the old log building in 1953 with a more modern

"International-style" station, boasting its trademark, low flat roof. The architects made use of stone around the base and in the wide chimney, while the station name was created in individual letters above the roof, as with many such International-style stations. While the yards now sit largely empty and most divisional structures such as the roundhouse have gone, a few buildings linger in the quiet residential townsite, including a water tower, a telegraph building, and a crew rest house. Although designated under the HRSPA in 1995, the station now sits vacant.

Fort Langley, B.C. (CNoR)

One of the few buildings erected according to CNoR plan 100-64 to survive, this two-storey pyramid-roofed station now houses the Fort Langley museum. It retained an agent until 1972, when it became a flag stop. Passenger service ended in 1980. Three years later, the Langley Heritage Society and the local municipality

The one-time CNoR station in Langley, British Columbia, now preserved, was built using that line's standard style, with its iconic pyramid roofline.

The CPR's log station at Glacier, British Columbia, recalls the days when passengers disembarked for skiing adventures. Although a heritage-designated structure, it is off-limits to the public.

moved the building to Mavis Street and Glover Road in Fort Langley.

Fraser Mills, B.C. (CPR)

Now located in the Heritage Square in Coquitlam B.C., the Fraser Mills CPR station was one of hundreds built by the CPR in its single-storey wooden style with a bell-cast roof that extended around the structure. It was built in 1910 and closed in 1970. Relocated at first in the 1970s to Blue Mountain Park, it was once again relocated in 1999, finding its way to Heritage Square.

Glacier, B.C. (CPR)

This delightful building is a rare surviving on-site example of the CPR's mountain log stations, designed to appeal specifically to the tourist trade, especially those headed to the nearby Glacier House resort (now demolished). It was built in 1916 near the western approach to the new Connaught Tunnel. Single-storey, it displays a large gable above the operator's bay window as well as a bay window at the eastern end of the waiting room. The station sits at the foot of the Illecillewaet Glacier in the Selkirk Mountains, and remains one the most scenic contexts of any Canadian station. Although designated under the HRSPA, it remains on CPR property, now vacant, and visits by the public are not encouraged.

Golden, B.C. (CPR)

Built in 1904 to a distinctive CPR plan, the storey-and-a-half wooden CPR station sits behind the Golden Museum and Archives on 13th Street. It retains its two-tone, maroon-and-yellow paint scheme and shows three hip dormers in the split-level, bell-cast roof. Restoration on the structure was underway in 2015. The VIA station, which replaced it, now serves as a Chamber of Commerce office.

The attractive CPR station in Golden, British Columbia, has been relocated to become a museum.

The former G&W station in Grand Forks, British Columbia, shows its distinctive American architectural style.

Grand Forks, B.C. (C&WR/CPR)

The storey-and-half station on the fringes of the community of Grand Forks was built by the Columbia and Western Railway in 1900 in order to capture business from the mining and agricultural industries of the region close to the U.S. border. The route was assumed by the CPR in 1905. Architects describe its features as being "Swiss Chalet–style" in form, consisting of a steep roof with prominent dormers, and a single-storey extension for the freight shed. No other similar railway structures survive. The station itself serves as a bar and restaurant. It was placed on the Canadian Register of Historic Places in 1991.

Jasper, AB (CNR)

The striking Jasper station was the CNR's response to the CPR's Banff and Lake Louise stations. It was built within the boundaries of Jasper National Park to serve the railway's Jasper Park Lodge. Designed in the CNR's Winnipeg architectural department, its rusticated features include cobblestone chimneys and wainscoting, heavy beamed ceilings, limestone, exposed rafters, and elegant lighting. The steeply sloping bell-cast roof contains two ski-slope gables flanking the stone, trackside entranceway. Designated in 1992 under the HRSPA, it continues to serve as VIA Rail's eastern terminal for the *Skeena* to Prince Rupert, as well as a stop for the transcontinental *Canadian* train. The *Rocky Mountaineer* tour train calls here as well.

Kamloops, B.C. (CNR)

Located in downtown Kamloops amidst an area of large-scale redevelopment, the CNR's Kamloops station was built in 1926 and designed by the rail line's own architectural department. The two-storey brick building rests on a stone base and has a pair of small gables in the roofline. Although CN trains now pass north of the South Thompson River, via Kamloops

The historic and elegant CNR station in Kamloops, British Columbia, is the boarding point for steam train excursions. Inside it is now a restaurant.

The former CNR station in Kelowna, like many, has now become a bar.

Junction, where the massive yards still operate, track still lies along the platform, but the only trains today are those of the Kamloops Heritage Railway steam train. Designated in 1992 under the HRSPA, the station now houses a Keg Restaurant and is the boarding point for the tour train.

Kelowna, B.C. (CNR)

The single-storey station in downtown Kelowna was constructed by the CNR in 1926 as the terminus on its Okanagan Valley branch line. It is simple in style: a single storey with an eyebrow gable on its roof. With the tracks now gone, and new development having moved in, there is little evidence that its former yards once stretched to the lake. The interior has been renovated to house a bar, although the exterior retains much of its original appearance. It was designated under the HRSPA in 1991.

Ladysmith, B.C. (E&N/CPR)

The single-storey former CPR station in Ladysmith lay on the Esquimalt and Nanaimo Railway line. It was constructed in 1944 to replace the original, two-storey, wooden E&N station built in 1901. Trains stopped calling in 2011 and the CPR leased the building to the municipality. It still stands, although it is now empty and boarded up. Behind it, the Ladysmith Railway Museum offers displays of early railway rolling stock.

Lake Cowichan, B.C. (E&N/CPR)

Now known as the Kaatza Station Museum, this former E&N station, built in 1913, was put up for sale in 1979 and four years later relocated a short distance away to become a local museum. The wooden building nicely preserves the style that the CPR adopted for many of its E&N-line stations on Vancouver Island, i.e., a single-storey wooden structure with an elevated freight shed. The museum's grounds, which also features two restored schools from early in the century, includes a display of early railway rolling stock, which includes two locomotives, a logging car, a speeder, and a caboose. The museum is on Kaatza Place in Lake Cowichan, near the shore of the lake.

Lake Louise, AB (CPR)

For the railways, nothing seemed to say "mountains" like log buildings. And the CPR used rustic log stations to lure tourists onto its trains to the mountains, in this case the Chateau Lake Louise. Built in 1910, the Lake Louise structure is built of log throughout, with a large stone fireplace in the former waiting rooms. Its three hearths served the three station areas: namely, the general waiting room, the ladies' waiting room, and the ticketing area. Large, leaded-glass windows, which extend into the high cross gables, afford mountain views in all directions. Designated a historic building in 1990 under the HRSPA, the Lake Louise station is now the Lake Louise Station Restaurant. Two historic passenger coaches parked adjacent to the building offer extra dining space. The parking lot behind the station is where travellers would board the trams to take them to the hotel and the lake.

McBride, B.C. (GTP)

Built in 1919, the McBride station was specially designed to serve as the GTP's divisional point on the Jasper to Prince Rupert line. The townsite was also laid out by the railway, as was the case in many places along its western lines, and reflects the usual grid pattern of streets. The two-storey, stuccoed building includes a hip-gable roof and dormers

The Lake Louise, Alberta, station is now a popular fine-dining restaurant.

on both track and street side. Otherwise, it offers no unusual architectural embellishments. The building came under the HRSPA in 1991 and in addition to offering a waiting room for VIA Rail's *Skeena* passengers, it now functions as the tourist information centre and contains a "beanery."

Midway, B.C. (CPR)

Another rare CPR survivor, the Midway station sits a few metres from its original location in the southern B.C. town of Midway. It was built in 1909 by the CPR according to its standard rural plan, with a two-storey main building and a hip dormer in the roof. It is today a station museum and Mile 0 for the Kettle Valley Rail Trail.

Nanaimo, B.C. (E&N/CPR)

For a time, Nanaimo served as the northern terminus for the Esquimalt and Nanaimo Railway (later the CPR). Built in 1916, the building represents an unusual

The station in Nanaimo, British Columbia, was one of the most elaborate on the E&N line.

The CPR's large station in Nelson, British Columbia, underwent extensive renovations to become a business and tourist centre.

variation upon the CPR's Plan 9 station style. The central portion consists of a two-storey block capped with a stepped-parapet gable. The exterior walls are covered with dark red shingles on the lower two-thirds while white stucco lies on the upper third. Tongue-in-groove walls, hardwood flooring, and a wooden staircase marked the interior. In 2006, a fire gutted much of the station. However, the building was restored in 2012, and for a time became home to Fibber Magees Station Irish Pub-Style Restaurant, (which closed in late 2015). Today, the structure (which still has a waiting room) awaits the possible restoration of train service.

Nelson, B.C. (CPR)

This large wooden station, rich in architectural details, was built by the CPR in 1900. Its role was two-fold: to provide a connection between the CPR and the steamships on Kootenay Lake to serve the growing mining industry in the region; and also to keep ahead of the

looming threat of American rail expansion into southern British Columbia. Two-and-half stories in height, the station has a roof embellished with a series of gables and dormers. The exterior displays half-timbered and stucco accents which continued into the 1910 additions. In 2015, the station, which no longer serves a railway function, although the rail yards remain in use, was being repurposed as a visitor and business centre for the city's refurbished historic main street.

Oliver, B.C. (CPR)

The CPR built the station in 1923, when the first passenger train puffed by, operating it only seasonally, until 1934 when it became permanent. The style is the standard CPR plan N4, common in rural communities throughout Canada. Rail service ended here in 1977 and the tracks came up two years later. In 1983, the town relocated and renovated the building, only to see it gutted by fire in 1988. After the fire, the single-storey wooden station near the main street of Oliver was restored and now serves as the Chamber of Commerce and tourist office. The Kettle Valley Rail Trail passes by its doors.

Parksville, B.C. (E&N/CPR)

The delightful wooden E&N station on Railway Street in Parksville follows the standard style used by the CPR on the E&N line on Vancouver Island. Built in 1913, the station, like its sister in Lake Cowichan, is a single-storey structure with a raised freight shed. Unlike any other station on Vancouver Island, however, it has retained its water tower, now part of a preservation effort. While it awaits its fate as a railway facility, it is home to the Arrowsmith Potters Guild.

Port Alberni, B.C. (E&N/CPR)

This heritage-designated CPR station, built for the E&N branch to Port Alberni, rises two stories in the central portion with single-storey extensions to each side. Built in 1911, it functioned as a station until 1970. Following its closure, the city purchased the building and restored it as a home for the Alberni Tourist Railway. It remains on its original site on Kingsway Avenue, near the waterfront. A water tower serves the steam locomotive for its excursions to the McLean Mill historic site. Freight service ended in 2001, although tracks remain in place for the remainder of the sixty-three kilometres to its junction with the E&N tracks at Parksville.

Port Moody, British Columbia, was briefly the CPR's western terminus. Its station is now a museum.

Port Moody, B.C. (CPR)

One of the CPR's most historic locations, Port Moody was the CPR's first West-Coast terminal, built before the railway relocated to a site farther west, near Gastown, which proved to have superior harbour access. Built in 1908, the station is the site's second such structure. In 1945, it was lifted from its foundation, placed on rail cars, and moved to a new, more central location on Queen Street. In 1978, after the CPR discontinued using it, the Port Moody Historical Society moved it to a new location to become the focus of the popular Port Moody Station Museum. Not a common CPR style, the red wooden building, built according to a design known as plan N9, displays a full second-floor cross gable, which originally housed the agent and his family. The interior contains the furnishings with which the agent would have been familiar in the 1920s and '30s. The station museum is situated at 2743 Murray Street.

Prince George, B.C. (CN/ Penny GTP)

Partway between Jasper and Prince Rupert on the CNR line, Prince George remains an active railway town. The modern two-storey station located on First Avenue is a key overnight stop for VIA Rail's scenic and popular *Skeena* train. It also serves CN Rail, which operates a major rail yard here.

Nearby, at the Prince George Railway Museum, sits the GTP station from the village of Penny. It was built to the common Plan E style, with its bell-cast roof and dormer inserted into the roofline directly above the operator's bay. This was the nearly universal style adopted by the GTP on its cross-country line. It was moved to the museum grounds in 1988. The original GTP station in Penny was built in 1914 but burned in 1947, at which time an identical station from Lindup was brought in to replace it.

The British Columbia Railway station was added to Prince George in 1952, after the line from Vancouver was eventually closed. When CNR took over the BCR, it abolished passenger service, and today the single-storey, glass-enclosed station is for rail operations only. It sits on Industrial Way at the south end of the town.

Prince Rupert, B.C. (CNR)

This ocean port can claim three railway stations, two of them historic, the third modern but still in railway service.

The Kwinitsa station sits by the waterfront, close to the former CNR station. Built in 1911 in the small community of Kwinitsa, between Prince Rupert and Terrace, it represents the most common station style designed by the Grand Trunk Pacific. These small buildings were but a single storey, although the steep roofline allowed for a small dormer above the agent's bay window, which was just room enough for an agent's apartment. More than one hundred such stations lined the route between Winnipeg and Prince Rupert. Only four are known to survive. It was brought to the waterfront in 1985 to become the Kwinista Railway Museum. The museum collection depicts the lives of railway families and the early railway history of Prince Rupert.

Nearby, and on its original site, is the 1922 CN station. Designed by the CN's architectural department in Winnipeg, this classical modern station, one of the CN's earliest in this style, is constructed of brick with limestone trim and displays a flat roof. Its two stories contained the offices of the CNR, as well as waiting rooms on the ground level. The building was designated a heritage structure under the HRSPA in 1992; however, since the relocation of VIA Rail to the new ferry docks, the building has nevertheless sat vacant.

The third of Prince Rupert's stations was its first GTP station — a simple wooden structure with a passenger shed for those awaiting transfer to coastal steamers. Apart from the station, a string of factories lined the tracks. A steel walkway led across the tracks to the station from the town located on a bank high above.

Qualicum Beach, B.C. (E&N/CPR)

When the Esquimalt and Nanaimo Railway reached Qualicum Beach in 1914, it added a station to lure tourists to this oceanside retreat. The wooden station reflects a style not found elsewhere along this line but common in eastern Canada. It is a storey-and-a-half wooden building

The CNR's original terminal station in Prince Rupert, British Columbia, is a designated heritage station, even though it is currently boarded up.

with a hip dormer punctuating the steep bell-cast roofline. Twin dormers appear on the street side, the single dormer on the track side. The red wooden station, which is located in a rural setting some distance from the tourist town itself, claims wood-shingle roofing and clapboard siding.

The building was leased to the town in 1988 and restored to house space for community groups as well as storage for the town. It was designated under the HRSPA in 1994 and served VIA Rail until service was suspended in 2011. It has since been restored as a heritage building.

Revelstoke, B.C. (CPR)

As with many of the CPR's first-generation stations across the nation, Revelstoke's first CPR station was the standard, hurriedly built, "Van Horne" style structure: a wooden, two-storey style with peak-gable ends. (The Van Hornes were so named after William Cornelius Van Horne, the CPR's feisty general manager and, later,

president, who chose a single, simple station plan that could be shipped along the line to local contractors who would build them.)

Once the Van Hornes had served their start-up purpose, the CPR quickly substituted more elegant stations. When the CPR added a branch line from Revelstoke to the Arrow Lakes in 1893, it relocated its divisional facilities from Donald to Revelstoke and in 1899 added a new divisional station. An extended two-storey building, the new building was made mostly of brick, although it featured a stone base and stone highlights on the corners. The arched windows reflected the Richardsonian influence then being employed by station architects of the day. Two-storey end sections extended beyond the main structure while the canopy wrapped around the entire building.

In 1978, the fine old divisional station, by no means on its last legs, was replaced with a more modern, rather featureless two-storey concrete slab. Not considered a heritage building, it serves as the main offices for the railway's Revelstoke operations and a stop for the *Rocky Mountaineer* tour train.

Salmo, B.C. (GNR)

Designated a heritage station in 1992, the storey and a half wooden station in Salmo was constructed by the Great Northern Railway (now the Burlington Northern and Santa Fe Railway) in 1913 in an effort to compete with the Canadian Pacific Railway which was then soon to dominate southern British Columbia. As with most American designed stations, the Salmo station is a simple wooden structure with no real architectural embellishments. The line was abandoned in 1989 and the road bed has become the popular although rugged Great Northern Rail Trail. Parks Canada describes the building as "one of the best surviving examples of a standard GNR depot in Canada." The building remains in its original site and largely in original condition at the end of the town's historical main street, and south of Nelson B.C. on Highway 6.

Salmon Arm, B.C. (CPR)

Many years have passed since a passenger train last stopped at the CPR's Salmon Arm station. The building is one of the few original stations in western Canada to remain in railway use. Built in 1913, this single storey wooden station with its wide sloping hip roof and still sporting its Tuscan red paint scheme has never been designated as a heritage building (although it clearly should be). It stands a block away from the town's busy main street and a short distance from a new waterfront park.

Smithers, B.C. (GTP)

Constructed in 1919, the atypical Grand Trunk Pacific station in Smithers, B.C., was one of the last built by the company before its bankruptcy. Its two-and-a-half storey size indicates it was intended for use as a divisional station. Its construction six years after the arrival of the railway marked the beginning of the community and remains the oldest structure in town. It displays various elements including varying colours and materials on a concrete base with brick walls and a stuccoed second storey. Structural variety includes bell-cast eaves, a steep hip bell-cast roof, as well as its large size. Waiting rooms and a dining hall occupied the main level, while divisional

The GTP's Smithers, British Columbia, station is a National Historic Site.

offices and accommodation filled the second and third floors. Designated in 1993, today it houses the Smjthers Community Services Association. VIA Rail's *Skeena* still stops, but the station no longer fills the role of furnishing tickets or providing a waiting room.

Terrace, B.C. (CN)

If the VIA station in Terrace looks more like a house, it was. At least at first. Anticipating growth from the pending arrival of the Grand Trunk Pacific Railway, George Little had acquired a tract of land beside the proposed tracks of the Grand Trunk Pacific Railway and on those sixty hectares surveyed out what would become the town of Terrace. Little granted a portion of that land to the GTP for a station, thus ensuring the growth of his town plan.

Built in 1914, the Little house was the largest in the fledgling community. As the town grew, the house was sold and moved, more than once actually. In 2003, in order to honour the town's founder and to encourage growth and tourism, the Ksan House Society, the then owners, donated the building to the city which moved it to the tracks. It replaced a 1950s-era CNR station with a low, sloping roof and glass-and-steel walls. The original GTP station was named the Littleton station, after founder George Little (it was soon changed to Terrace as there already was a station named Littleton) and was the typical 100-52 plan for the GTP's smaller locations. Today, the storey-and-a-half wooden house serves as a VIA station stop and gift shop which includes the work of local artists.

Valemount, B.C. (CNoR)

Now moved from its original site, the Canadian Northern's station now serves as a community museum. Among the displays are a mock-up of a trapper's cabin, railway lanterns, a restored agents' bedroom, early farm equipment, station kitchen, pioneer items, and a model railway layout, while outside a steel caboose is equipped with contemporary furnishings. The station was built by the CNoR in 1915 according to its 100-98 plan. Unlike the railway's stations with the iconic pyramid roof design, this is a more scaled-down building, with two stories, peak gables on the ends, and a pair of simple dormers in the roofline. Originally opened in Swift Creek, it was moved to its location in Valemount in 1927. It served as a station until 1981 before being relocated a short distance from the tracks and opened as the Valemount Museum in 1992. A similar station still stands by the highway in Hope.

The CPR's third station in Vancouver, a heritage-designated structure, retains a transportation role as the terminus for intercity rail service and ferry service. Its interior features have been nicely preserved.

Vancouver's Grand Terminals
CPR

When CPR steam locomotive #347 puffed into the CPR's new Vancouver station in 1887, it arrived at a modest wooden building overlooking Burrard Inlet. But within two years the dynamic CPR general manager, William Cornelius Van Horne, embarked on the construction of the finest station on his western main line. The new structure, designed by the CPR's main architect, Edward Maxwell, soared above the street in a chateau style with a high, peaked roof and grand, arched entranceway. Soaring seven and a half stories, the station culminated in a pyramid roof flanked by a pair of four-storey towers. Flanking the stone entrance stood a pair of two-and-a-half-storey wings.

Alas, with the boom in Vancouver's growth, the building quickly proved to be inadequate, and by 1912 a new, classical-style station was under construction. Designed by Barrott, Blackadar, and Webster, this three-storey, neo-classical brick station filled an entire city block and boasted ten two-storey columns. Still standing, the station features a two-storey waiting room decorated by a series of paintings around the ceiling. In 1979, VIA's passenger service moved to an equally grand station on Main Street, one built by the Canadian Northern Railway. Meanwhile, the grandeur of the CPR station continues to greet passengers on the commuter trains, those arriving by ferry, or simply those wandering in for a meal in one of the cafes located inside.

CNoR

Located on Main Street, on the east side of Vancouver, near the east end of False Creek, were a pair of nearly twin terminal stations: one built by the Canadian Northern Railway in 1916; and one constructed by the Great Northern Railway around the same time. Both were "stub" stations — that is, the tracks ended at the rear of the buildings. Both were marked by grand entranceways and lofty waiting rooms.

The GNR station, built of brick, boasted a three-storey main section flanked on each side by two-storey wings. The entrance was through dual arched doorways at each end of the main section. The building lasted until 1965, when it was demolished, ostensibly over municipal taxes. The railway then moved in with the CNR station, until GNR service ended in 1969.

Designed in the beaux-arts style, the station features a grand, three-storey arch that marks the towered entrance to Canadian Northern's two-storey waiting room. Above the arch sits a classical parapet resting atop two Doric columns. Encircling the waiting room were a ticket office, a lunch counter, a telegraph office,

VIA Rail's popular cross-country *Canadian ends its run at Vancouver's heritage-designated CNR station.*

and baggage room. Travellers could walk in the front entrance and then proceed directly to the boarding platforms. Longer passenger trains had to be turned in stages in order to face the departing position. The CNoR's own offices occupied the two upper floors.

Following the absorption of the CNoR by the CNR, that company's passenger service continued until the creation of VIA Rail, whose trains began to call in 1979. The large CANADIAN NATIONAL sign, which stood high above the roof, is gone now; in its place, an equally large, neon, PACIFIC CENTRAL sign stands. The station was designated as a heritage structure in 1991. Today it serves as a bus terminal and terminal for both VIA Rail's *Canadian* and Amtrak's *Cascades* train services. A U.S. Customs office in the station performs pre-boarding Customs clearances. Boasting a snack bar, a baggage room, and railway staff, the building still largely retains its function as a station. The waiting hall remains as grand as ever, with its traditional clock and ceiling fixtures and décor. Security guards, however, discourage photography inside.

The grand hall of the Vancouver station reflects the elegance of early station architecture. Today it serves as the embarkation point for VIA Rail's trains and for Amtrak trains to the United States, as well as for bus routes to various points in Canada and the United States.

White Rock, B.C. (BNSF)

This white, wooden, single-storey, former Great Northern Station was built in 1913 and sits on White Rock's ocean shoreline. Close to the U.S. border, the station served as a Customs point and contains a jail cell and immigration hall. The last train to stop there was in 1975, and in 1979 the station was donated to the City of White Rock, which designated it as a heritage building. Following its use by a variety of occupants, it has housed the White Rock Museum and Archives since 1990. Trains still rumble past, but no longer stop. These may include Amtrak's *Cascades* passenger train and the *Rocky Mountaineer*, as well as freight trains.

SAVING OUR STATIONS; PRIVATE PRESERVATION EFFORTS

Across the mountains and through the Canadian West, not all historic stations have received heritage protection. Here, many private groups and individuals have, on their own, striven to salvage the West's railway heritage by repurposing redundant railway stations.

Abbotsford, B.C. (CPR)

In the 1980s, when the CPR Type-12 station in Abbotsford, a two-storey, pyramid-roofed station with hip-gable dormer was threatened with demolition, the owners of Heritage Valley Resort in Clayburn disassembled the building and relocated it to become the office for the facility. The exterior of the building retains all its railway features.

Hope, B.C. (CN)

Hope's CN station was built by the CNoR in 1916 with the intention of sharing it with the Vancouver, Victoria, and Eastern Railway. The rare style, known as Plan 100-84, consists of a storey-and-a-half central block with two dormers in the roof indicating the apartment of the station agent, and two single extensions to either side. It was moved from its original site to a location beside Highway 5 where it has served as a restaurant and arts centre.

New Westminster, B.C. (BCER)

Directly across the road from the elegant CPR station is the equally significant British Columbia Electric Railway terminal. The BCER was an interurban commuter line that ran between New Westminster and Chilliwack starting in 1910. The terminal was designed by the firm of McClure and Fox and opened in 1911.

The BCER ended operations in 1950, at which time the downtown terminal was converted to commercial uses and its facade covered over. More recently, the original brick facade has been restored, but walking through the repurposed interior, among the racks of dresses and shirts and other apparel, it is hard to believe there was once a busy set of streetcar tracks, or that the atmosphere was once dominated by the smell of grease and oil, although the archways through which the streetcars moved are still evident. The building was added to the Canadian Register of Historic Places in 2004. The building sits on Columbia Street, at the western end of the city's historic downtown.

New Westminster, B.C. (CPR)

This attractive, chateau-style station was designed by the CPR's favourite architect, Edward Maxwell, and built in 1899 following a fire that destroyed much of downtown New Westminster. It replaced the first station, a wooden structure, built in 1886 when the CPR first came to town. The current building was added to the Canadian Register of Historic Places in 2005. A steep, two-storey gable rises above the arched, streetside entrance, while a pair of turrets guard the trackside entrance. The building material is brick, with stone trim. While tracks remain nearby, the earlier tracks are now a busy roadway. The building now houses a restaurant and sits across the street from the former BCER station.

The CPR's station in New Westminster, British Columbia, reflects that company's penchant for the chateau style of architecture. It now contains a restaurant.

Osoyoos, B.C. (CPR)

This station, a single-storey, wooden CPR Plan N4, now sits by Okanagan Lake as the office for a sailing club.

Pemberton, B.C. (CN)

Despite its historic appearance, the CN station in this historic gold rush town is of recent construction and now houses a Greyhound bus depot and café. The much altered Pemberton Hotel stands immediately behind it. The Pemberton Museum, which is within walking distance of the station, offers a collection which includes the railway heritage of the valley.

Penticton, B.C. (CPR)

Built on line of the Kettle Valley Railway in 1941 by the CPR, amid what were then the Penticton railyards, the two-storey Penticton divisional station now houses a variety

The unusual station in Penticton, British Columbia, was once the centre of a busy rail yard. Today it is in a parking lot.

The station in Quesnel, British Columbia, is a Pacific Great Eastern Railway original, one of only two in this style to survive.

of service clubs. The once-busy yards have been replaced by suburban malls and parking lots. The two-storey building displays a pair of half-timber cross gables at each end of the structure. The structure became a designated heritage building in 2006. It is located on Hastings Avenue, well away from the waterfront where the original Penticton station once welcomed travellers on the lake steamers.

Princeton, B.C. (GNR)

Now a Subway restaurant, the Great Northern station in Princeton was built in 1915 as a standard single-storey building with a gable roof and octagonal bay. It remains on its original site and sits on a walking trail through town.

Quesnel, B.C. (PGER/BCR)

This two-storey station was built in a distinctive Pacific Great Eastern Railway style, similar to that in Williams Lake. It was built in 1921 and served as the line's northern terminal until 1952 when the PGER finally extended its tracks across the Cottonwood River and on to Prince George. The PGER was bought out by BC Rail in 1972. The station closed its doors in 2002, but more recently it has become an overnight stop for the *Rocky Mountaineer* tour train.

Vancouver, B.C. (BCER)

Located at the corner of Hastings and Carall streets in downtown Vancouver, a handsome stone-and-brick, "Second Empire Renaissance" style building served as the Vancouver terminal of the British Columbia Electric Railway. Designed by Sommervell and Putnam, it opened in 1911 and was the focus of what was at the time the most extensive interurban network in Canada. In addition to the public waiting room, the building housed more than three hundred workers. Its appearance is distinguished by arched windows on the ground floor and fenestrations that rise three storeys above that. The building is now occupied by Lightform. It was listed on the CRHP in 2003.

Vernon, B.C. (CPR)

When the CPR extended a branch line from Sicamous to Okanagan Landing to open up the Okanagan Valley in 1891, it built a station in the fledgling community of Vernon. But by 1911, that little community was booming, and the CPR added one of its western-plan brick stations, a diminutive version of those that it had added in Lethbridge and Saskatoon among others. It was built of brick over a limestone foundation, with granite trim, and an octagonal turret on the street with a half-timber gable above the operator's bay by the tracks. By 1973, the CPR had centralized its operations in the new Revelstoke station, and the Vernon station was leased to private interests. Today it houses the Station BBQ Smokehouse. Vernon's first CPR station was relocated to the outskirts of the city, where it now forms part of a local community centre.

Williams Lake, B.C. (PGER/BCR)

Similar in style and age to its twin in Quesnel, the former Pacific Great Eastern station in Williams Lake now houses the Station House Gallery and Gift Shop, a group that formed in 1981 to preserve and repurpose the two-storey wooden building. The Williams Lake station, along with that in Quesnel, represents the only two surviving first-generation PGE stations in British Columbia. In true railway fashion, the former station lies at the end of the main street. Highways 97 and 20 both meet in Williams Lake.

LIFE ON THE LINE: THE RAILWAY TOWNS

Unlike the string of railside towns and villages that grew around the Prairie stations, few towns along the mountain rail lines developed into sizable communities. The railways, after all, were awarded sizable land grants along their Prairie lines upon which to create towns of their own. They had full control over the shape of those communities. Streets were laid out in a grid network with the main street conveniently ending at the rear of the station.

However, in the steep valleys and hard mountainous terrain of western Alberta and British Columbia, there was little opportunity for development. Stations were often isolated outposts, snowed in by drifts that could bury the buildings, and occasionally did. Some, such as the CPR station in the Rogers Pass, were buried beneath deadly avalanches and had to be moved.

Town growth fared better along the Grand Trunk Pacific, in the farmlands of the lower Fraser area, and on Vancouver Island. In the mountains, the mineral bounty of silver, zinc, and coal spawned boom towns, whose primary outside links were those created by the rail lines. Otherwise,

the only places to attain any size were the divisional towns. These occurred every 150 kilometres or so, and were built to provide crew changes, locomotive maintenance, and coaling and sanding towers. Most had modest accommodation for the crews — often simply a bunkhouse; more rarely, houses; perhaps a hotel or dining hall for travellers, and housing for ancillary businesses and railway managers.

THE CPR DIVISIONAL TOWNS: THE MAIN LINE

Field, B.C.
Field began its role as a divisional town in 1909. From its origins as head of track during construction, it filled a key role as the base for locomotives helping haul freights up the "Big Hill," located to the east between Field and Hector. With a track gradient twice that of normal (4.5 percent versus 2.2 percent), the hill proved an obstacle until 1909 when the famous Spiral Tunnels were completed. After the Spiral Tunnels opened,

reducing the grade to the requisite 2.2 percent, the CPR moved its divisional point from Laggan to Field and added a roundhouse, station, water tower, coal dock, housing for the crew, and a dining station known as the Mount Stephen House.

The town sits in the middle of Yoho National Park, which was created at the instigation of Van Horne to further help lure wealthy world travellers. (Field was named hopefully for an American Cyrus Field from whom the CPR vainly sought investment capital). As with the newly named Lake Louise, the area quickly became a tourist destination with the Mount Stephen House Hotel and nearby skiing. In 1918, with tourists swarming to Lake Louise and Banff, the hotel became a railway YMCA and lasted until 1954 when it was demolished.

Today, a few vestiges remain. Still standing high above the townsite is the black-iron water tower. A new inn, constructed of log, has replicated the style of the older hotel, a few renovated former crew houses line the streets, and a telegraph house still stands near the tracks. While the station stands vacant, and the yards are largely empty, a new bunkhouse, renovated in 1999, offers accommodation for the train crews. Vestiges of the stone roundhouse lasted until the 1990s.

Golden, B.C.

The town with the glittery name owes its origins to a CPR surveyors' camp, and its name (initially Golden City) to its desire to outclass a rival CPR camp named Silver City. In 1907, when the Kootenay Central Railway extended a branch line south from Golden to meet the CPR's southern main route at Fort Steele Junction, it became an important railway junction, adding an engine house, a water tank, and a large, two-storey station. While the water tank and many of the sidings have gone, the station rests in a new location at the town's museum. Near the station's original site, a former standard VIA station shelter now houses the chamber of commerce, while across the street a one-time railway bunkhouse now houses the Dreamcatcher Hostel and a nearby former railway hotel has become business offices. The landscaped main street yet retains early buildings from the town's early days of rail.

Kamloops, B.C.

The modern city of Kamloops, located at the junction of the North and South Thompson Rivers, can lay claim to being not one but two divisional points — both for the CPR, and, later, for the Canadian Northern Pacific Railway. The first was built when the CPR arrived in 1885. Although Kamloops had for years been a busy riverside fur-trading post, the arrival of the CPR and its tracks running right down the town's main street, spurred its growth into a city, which it formally became in 1893. The location contained the usual roundhouse, water tower, and large divisional station. The CPR's heritage has pretty well vanished, however, as the downtown has expanded and become revitalized. The roundhouse and tower are gone, and the original station has been replaced by a 1959 modern structure. This location remains a busy divisional and crew change point for the railway.

Lake Louise, AB

As the CPR rail builders laid track west from Calgary in the early 1880s, Canmore became the CPR's first mountain divisional point west of Calgary. Then, in 1899, the railway moved the function to Laggan, as Lake Louise was then called. With a six-stall engine house, water tower, and wye, it retained this role until the Spiral Tunnels opened in 1909, when the function moved, once again, to Field.

The original Laggan station, built of log, stands today in the Calgary Heritage Park. In 1909, a new, larger, log station was built, to enhance the appeal of the tourist attraction then being created on the shores of the spectacular mountain-bound Lake Louise. Following the opening of the Lake Louise Hotel in 1912, a narrow-gauge tramway shuttled passengers six kilometres from the train station up a steep hill to the hotel. That route is now a 4.8-kilometre trail known as the Tramway Trail. Today, that elegant log replacement has become a popular fine dining restaurant, with a display of vintage passenger coaches beside it. VIA Rail's passenger trains called until 1990, when the trains were booted off the CPR's lines and onto those of the CNR.

North Bend, B.C.

The CPR created this divisional point, now almost a ghost town, on a flat terrace beside the fast-flowing Fraser River. Here, in 1886, the railway built the Fraser Canyon House as a stop for tourists enthralled with the mountain scenery. A stone roundhouse and employee housing completed the site. A second hotel, the Mountain Hotel, was replaced in 1935 and lasted until the 1970s, when it burned.

North Bend remains a crew-change location today. A new bunkhouse tends to the train crews' needs, while a more modern station has replaced the old one. The town also remains a small residential community, with a number of small homes dating to the CPR's divisional days. In 1913, the CPR built a string of eight high-line houses on a hillside well away from the tracks, of which only two remain. However, a number of smaller homes nearer the tracks date from the days when the town was a busy divisional point.

Revelstoke, B.C.

Tucked into the valley between the Selkirk and the Monashee mountain ranges sits one of British Columbia's busiest railway divisional points: Revelstoke. A surveyor named A.S. Farwell had selected the location as early as 1880 for a townsite, naming it after himself. As many land owners did, Farwell tried to exact an exorbitant price from CPR for his land. But as many railways did, the CPR decided to choose a more distant location for its station, namely east of Farwell's planned townsite and on the opposite side of the tracks. Not too surprisingly, Farwell disputed the CPR's claim to the land, and development of the site did not proceed until 1899, when the CPR relocated its divisional point from Donald. In the meantime, a string of hotels and bawdy houses lined the tracks, giving the place what one commentator called a "Wild West" atmosphere.

In 1886, with the inauguration of transcontinental train service, the CPR renamed its location Revelstoke, after England's Lord Revelstoke, one of the CPR's main financiers. Just three years later, the railway established a branch line to the Arrow Lakes and made the place a key railway junction; in 1899, it upgraded it to serve as a divisional point. In 1905, the CPR erected a large, two-storey divisional headquarters, which survived until 1978, when a more modern station was built in its place. In 1980, a new diesel shop replaced the eighteen-stall roundhouse.

As the town grew with the railway, it acquired an opera house and department store, along with a YMCA to offer accommodation for the train crews. A Customs house checked passengers and freight arriving from the United States via the Arrow Lakes.

Although VIA Rail no longer calls, the popular *Rocky Mountaineer* tour train does pause at this location, but not long enough for its passengers to enjoy the rejuvenated main street and its heritage buildings, many of which date to the arrival of the railway over the mountains. Most of the railway activity centres on the extensive yards southeast of the town centre, while at the far north end of the yards, a popular railway museum displays early rolling stock and retells the story of the town's railway history. Other than that, the town has retained few vestiges of its early railway heyday.

Vancouver, B.C.

From a crude sawmill town on the shores of Burrard Inlet, Vancouver became the western terminus of the National Dream, the Canadian Pacific Railway.

After considerable survey work, the CPR concluded that its best option for its western leg was to follow the Fraser River Canyon to a spot on Burrard Inlet known as Port Moody. But, after constructing docks and a simple wooden station there, the CPR realized that the channel to the terminus was too shallow and decided, instead, to extend the route farther west to a better harbour location.

Two competing locations came up. English Bay had a superior land base for CPR facilities and was promoted by land speculators. The other, at Hastings Mill, was promoted by business interests from the rollicking little settlement nearby known as Gastown.

To fool the land speculators, the CPR let on that the English Bay route was its preferred option. Indeed, it surveyed the area there and built tracks. However, in the end it opted for Hastings Mill, where it installed its station and yards. By 1887, when locomotive #374 puffed into town with the CPR's first transcontinental passenger train behind it, the town had been surveyed and building was booming. (#371 had actually arrived at Port Moody a year earlier).

It did however find the English Bay branch useful for locating a roundhouse and other yard facilities, which they erected on the north side of False Creek. In the area near the roundhouse on Drake Street, the CPR workers were establishing their own community.

In 1900, after the CPR had established its major facilities north of False Creek, naming the area Yaletown after the former location in Yale, the City of Vancouver laid out an eight-block warehouse district to accommodate CPR freight shipments and zoned the area for commercial and light industry. Warehousing and tracks took over the streets, where raised platforms allowed for the ease of loading. Canopies covered the platforms to protect goods and workers from the incessant winter rains of the West Coast. Rows of workers' housing were constructed, interspersed with the warehouses.

The 1950s witnessed increasing truck traffic, and the warehousing moved to more convenient highway locations, leaving the Yaletown warehouse district to decline. The English Bay branch line was abandoned and most of the Drake Street facilities were replaced by newer developments, especially during the construction of the modern buildings to serve the exposition known as Expo 86, or TransExpo.

At the same time, the warehouse district was being "discovered" as a convenient and inexpensive place to live and do business, and the transformation began. Warehouses and working-class homes were made over into shops, lofts, and trendy restaurants. With the local buildings' surviving high-level loading ramps and cantilevered canopies built for the freight cars, the area displays a unique appearance and has been designated as a heritage district by the city for these unique features. These features are well displayed on a number of streets in the area, including Hamilton and Maitland streets. The nearby well-preserved Drake Street roundhouse is now a community centre, beside which a glass pavilion encloses that historic transcontinental steam locomotive #374.

However, the English Bay branch, which was used as a streetcar line until 1958, has all but vanished, although the Dunsmuir Tunnel, built in 1932 to carry the few trains to the Kitsilano terminal, is now used by Vancouver's SkyTrain commuter trains.

Today, Vancouver's third CPR station has become a terminal for the SeaBus ferry from North Vancouver as well as TransLink's West Coast Express commuter train service. Extensive rail yards remain in use behind the structure.

CPR'S SOUTHERN MAIN-LINE DIVISIONAL TOWNS

Brookmere, B.C.

This little near–ghost town may well be one of British Columbia's more intriguing railway divisional points. It attained this status due to the location of not just one, but two, rail lines there: the Kettle Valley Railway (operated by the CPR) and the Great Northern Railway (operating as the Vancouver, Victoria, and Eastern Railway). Here, the KVR added a turntable, a three-stall engine house (later replaced with a four-stall roundhouse by the CPR), a coal tipple, and crew accommodation. Since this was a two-sided station, it had a water tank with two spouts to serve the two lines. With the end of train service in 1961, Brookmere faded. Today it is a stop on the KVR Rail Trail. The water tank survives, as does a section house with the station nameboard. A caboose serves as a stop-over for trail users on the Kettle Valley Rail Trail. The site lies along the Clearwater Road east of Highway 5 and south of Merritt.

While not a ghost town, the nearby town of Coalmont, located southeast of Brookmere, offers a variety of heritage buildings along its historic but quiet main street, including the old hotel. However, being largely a former mining town, its railway heritage is negligible. It can be accessed by following the KVR Trail from Brookmere or the Coalmont Road from Princeton.

Northwest from Brookmere, the CPR line split, with one portion going south to join the CPR main line at Hope via the treacherous Coquihalla Canyon, the other swinging north to another main-line junction at Spences Bridge, where the CP established extensive car yards, a coal shed, and a water tank, although it was not considered a divisional point. Despite its former importance, no evidence of the community's railway roots remains.

The Great Northern Railway, part of the KVR/CPR network, erected an engine house and turntable at Hope in 1916 when the tracks finally met those of the CPR main line. These facilities however lasted only until 1930, and no trace remains.

Cranbrook, B.C.

If the railways needed any natural resource besides water, it was coal. Where the coal fields lay, the railways arrived. The extensive beds of coal that lay beneath the Crowsnest Pass in southwestern Alberta attracted the attention of one Colonel James Baker, who in 1886 established the Crow's Nest and Kootenay Lake Railway, whose purpose was to access the coal fields near Fernie. The CPR, not surprisingly, acquired the line and in 1898 created the divisional town of Cranbrook as part of its southern main line, bypassing the larger and older community of Fort Steele. Here they erected a sixteen-stall roundhouse, a water tower, a large station, and extensive yards. A grid network of streets stretched to the south of the tracks, while railway workers' homes were on the north side.

The new station collapsed in 1905 when a third floor was being added, but it was quickly repaired. After the Second World War, the station was completely remodelled — the new incarnation was an international-style structure with the standard flat roof, bearing little resemblance to its earlier form.

Despite this change, a great deal of Cranbrook's railway history remains. In fact, as a heritage site, Cranbrook is like no other. It has retained not only the station (now vacant) but the roundhouse, a freight shed, and a water tower, now relocated a short distance and preserved as a heritage feature. While the yards remain busy, the divisional functions have removed to Fort Steele Junction.

The treasure of the town, though, is one of western Canada's best railway museums and passenger train displays. Here the city has designated the "Railway Heritage Area." The district includes the historic ALCO diesel units; the Elko CPR station; the wooden water tower; the remodelled 1898 CPR station; the 1898 CPR freight shed; the museum building, containing the grand Royal Alexandra Hall from Winnipeg's 1906 CPR hotel, the remarkable train set displays, which are a National Historic Site, the Van Horne Gardens, named for the CPR president responsible for the completion of the railway, and the Prestige Rocky Mountain Resort, built adjacent to the tracks and host of the former CPR sleeper car, the Naughton, now used by the hotel guests. Adjacent to the heritage district, but not accessible to the public, lies the 1920 CPR roundhouse, and the site of previous structures such as the former railway YMCA, the ice houses, and the locations of workers' housing. Along with Vancouver's "warehouse" district, it is the only municipal designation specifically for a railway-related part of a city.

Midway, B.C.

Midway began life as a stage stop along the old Dewdney Trail, a once-busy stagecoach route. With the building of the Vancouver, Victoria, and Eastern Railway and the extension of the CPR's Columbia and Western Railway in 1906, it became a railway junction point as well. Once the CPR completed the KVR in 1916, it became an important divisional point on the CPR's southern main line. The yards, roundhouse, and other facilities were situated to the west of the town. The former yards are bare now. Only the standard two-storey CPR station survived the 1978 closing of the line; today it is a museum and serves as the trailhead for the Kettle Valley Rail Trail.

Nelson, B.C.

Tucked away in the cloudy mountains of British Columbia's southern Kootenay region, Nelson was established following the discovery of silver amid the lofty peaks. The province actively sought a railway connection from both the CPR, and the Great Northern Railway's Nelson and Fort Sheppard Railway. The CPR's Columbia and Kootenay Railway was the first to arrive, running from a steamer port on the Columbia River in 1891; the N&FS arrived two years later.

As the CPR continued to expand in the Kootenays in 1899, it established the growing community as its operational headquarters, adding a large, wooden, two-and-a-half-storey station as well as a roundhouse, and a shipyard for its vessels accessing the settlements around Kootenay Lake. As it grew, Nelson boasted the first streetcar system west of Winnipeg. A new roundhouse opened in the 1920s, which was replaced with a diesel repair shop in the 1950s with the end of steam. Today, a revitalized heritage main street leads to the large station, which is undergoing restoration in 2015, while the reactivated heritage tram line now rumbles along a waterfront park. As of 2015, the impressive wooden station was undergoing restoration as a business and tourist centre.

THE CANADIAN NORTHERN PACIFIC RAILWAY DIVISIONAL TOWNS

Basically, the name Canadian Northern Pacific Railway was the proper name of the western portion of the vast Canadian Northern Railway network. From Jasper, the CNoR made its way down the valley of Thompson River establishing divisional points at Blue River, Kamloops North, and Boston Bar, before making its way into Vancouver

Blue River, B.C.

With the arrival of the CNoR in 1915, the community of Blue River became a divisional point. The town contained a crew bunkhouse, a roundhouse, and a large standard CNoR divisional station, as well as a hotel and general store. With the replacement of steam with diesel, the divisional facilities were no longer required. The roundhouse and bunkhouse were removed, while the hotel eventually burned. For a number of years, the classic CNoR standard divisional station (similar to that at Boston Bar) served as a bed and breakfast, but it no longer stands. The newly renovated general store, built in 1912, still functions across from the site of the station. Other than the store, the sidings, and the standard grid street pattern, little of Blue River's railway heritage has survived.

Boston Bar, B.C.

For the CNoR's entire route down the Fraser Canyon, its tracks stood on the opposite bank from those of the CPR. So the railway must have had a similar location in mind for its divisional point as the CPR whose railway established its own divisional facilities at North Bend. Here, at Boston Bar, which stands directly across the river from North Bend, the CNoR established its own divisional point.

That did not occur, however, until 1915, when that ambitious railway company was creating a cross country network of its own. Here were the usual facilities of roundhouse, crew quarters, and large yards, with employee housing on a small network of streets behind.

Most of the structures are long gone. However, the classical CNoR divisional station still stands, proposed for use as a museum. Today, the Trans-Canada Highway cuts through the community bringing with it the usual roadside clutter of gas stations and restaurants. The train crews still change shifts here but in a newer bunkhouse. The highway has also brought a bridge that links the twin towns, replacing a one-car aerial cable car.

Kamloops, B.C.

North of the CP facilities, on the North Thompson River, the Canadian Northern Pacific Railway — part of the Canadian Northern Railway system — created another divisional point, with the water tank and standard CNoR pyramid-roof station. It also extended a branch across the bridge over the South Thompson into the centre of the city, where in 1927 the CNR, which had earlier assumed the assets of the bankrupt CNoR, erected a grand, two-storey brick station — the station still stands (it is now a Keg Restaurant). Because CNoR's railway workers were shuttled from the city to the more distant divisional location, no townsite ever developed around the CNoR's first station. That station no longer stands; in its place, a standard modern VIA station has been erected.

The yards, however, remain busy and contain a number of newer structures to serve the rolling stock, including a new facility and storage yards for the *Rocky Mountaineer* trains.

Vancouver, B.C.

In the beginning, Mackenzie and Mann intended to establish their West Coast yards and create a new town in Port Mann. However, falling land prices and a stagnant population changed their plans and they joined with the Great Northern Railway to share running rights in to Vancouver itself. In 1916, the CNoR finally rumbled into Vancouver, constructing its yards and erecting its grand classical station near Main Street. Beside it, the GNR built an equally attractive terminal of its own (demolished in the 1960s).

Being distant from Vancouver's burgeoning downtown core, a string of hotels grew along the street near the stations, many of them housing the railway crews. While the rail yards remain busy and the station provides services for VIA Rail, Amtrak, and bus routes, much of the surrounding area has experienced new growth and there is little else to remind anyone of the area's railway roots.

THE GRAND TRUNK PACIFIC DIVISIONAL TOWNS

Rejecting the notion of following the CNoR and CPR into Vancouver, the GTP opted for a more direct route to the Pacific Ocean, namely northwesterly from Jasper to Prince Rupert. Several towns along the Yellowhead Highway between Jasper and Prince Rupert began as divisional towns on the GTP. Among the best preserved are Smithers and McBride, both of which retain their historic stations and remain stops for VIA's *Skeena* train service. Endako, located between Smithers and Terrace, today consists of only a few buildings along the highway, belying its original role as a busy divisional point with yards, a roundhouse, a bunkhouse, and the line's highest railway water tower. The former railway hotel, originally known as the Grand Annan Hotel, is now the Endako Pub. Terrace became a divisional point with the relocation of that function from Pacific (now a ghost town). Here the interesting and historic George Little House now functions as the station for the town.

McBride, B.C.

Like the other communities along the Yellowhead Highway, McBride traces its roots to the coming of the GTP. After the surveyors laid out the town in 1912, the tracks appeared. The town was named in honour of then B.C. premier Richard McBride. In typical GTP fashion, the railway designed a townsite that consisted of a grid network of streets, with the main street ending at the back door of the station.

Little remains today of the yard structures, although a few of the sidings remain in use. A modern crew bunkhouse offers rest for the train crews that still change shifts here. The designated heritage station contains the Whistle Stop Gallery, a tourist information office, and a "beanery," an early railway term for a modestly priced restaurant. The refurbished hotel, which served the railway clientele, stands nearby. Today, the rail roots are largely forgotten, as visitors now stream past on the Yellowhead Highway, using the motels and fast food outlets that line that busy route.

The Princes ... Rupert and George, B.C.

Named for British royalty, as were many of Canada's western towns on the Grand Trunk Pacific Railway, the two towns were key points on the GTP rail line.

Prince Rupert was intended to serve as an important connection between the railway and the GTP's shipping line. The original proposed terminal was to have been at Port Simpson, a few kilometres to the north. But during the controversial boundary dispute, its location at the Alaska border compromised its security, and the location was moved farther south. Following its move, the town prospered. Its growth, although started by the railway terminal, developed on fishing and logging as well as freight and passenger shipping along the B.C. coast.

Little in the way of the town's railway heritage remains on display today. The designated CN station stands, now vacant, on the waterfront, while the small GTP standard-plan station from Kwinitsa now serves as a museum in a park beside it. The current VIA station was moved from the CN station into the more modern ferry terminal. A statue of Charles Melville Hays, president of the Grand Trunk Railway and founder of the town, stands by the city hall.

Prince George, by contrast, remains a busy divisional point for the CNR. Prior to the arrival of the GTP Railway, two communities vied for the GTP's proposed yards and station, namely Central Fort George and South Fort George. But, typically, the wily railway chose neither, opting for a townsite of its own, naming it Prince George. The community was laid out grid-like by the railway with the main artery leading from the station site to Princess Square. The only nod to town planning is a series of crescent streets said to be designed so as to isolate Central Fort George.

Alas, little railway heritage exists anymore, as much, including the large CN station, has been modernized, thanks to the building of the Yellowhead Highway. The BCR belatedly entered town from the south in the 1950s, but added little to the townscape, and the modern station is no longer used for passenger service. The VIA station, however, which shares the use of the CN building with the freight railway, sees the *Skeena* train overnight here three times a week in each direction.

The nearby Prince George Railway and Forestry Museum has become one of western Canada's leading railway displays.

Smithers, B.C.

Smithers is the next divisional point between Prince George and Terrace. Here, too, the usual divisional fixtures that would have once been found there, like the roundhouse, water tower, coal chute, and bunkhouses, are gone. The large, two-storey station today houses the Smithers Community Services Association as well as the VIA waiting room. The new CN yard office, located a short distance west, displays a pair of early CN logos on its walls. The grid street pattern is lined today with modern shops and homes. Little evidence of the original railway housing or businesses that once existed is found on them. As with McBride, the commercial focus is now along the Yellowhead Highway which passes along the north end of the community.

Terrace, B.C.

Although the town functioned as a GTP divisional point, other than the train yards, that heritage is in little evidence. The Yellowhead Highway passes through the town beside the tracks, meaning large modern businesses and big box stores stand where early railway-related buildings once were. The building that serves as the VIA station is a heritage house, known as the Little House, and was relocated from a different part of the town.

DIVISIONAL TOWNS ON THE PACIFIC GREAT EASTERN RAILWAY

For many years the Pacific Great Eastern Railway, later BC Rail (and now CN Rail), remained a "work in progress." Constructed from the port at Squamish, it reached Clinton in 1919 and Quesnel, where the tracks ended, later on. When the railway finally figured out how to conquer the Cottonwood Canyon, the line made its way northward, finally reaching its intended goal of Prince George in 1952.

Lillooet, B.C.

Situated at the mouth of a deep gorge in the Coast Mountains, Lillooet had long been a First Nations community. But when gold was discovered in the Fraser Canyon in 1858, Lillooet, along with Yale and Barkerville, became magnets for prospectors from across the country, booming into a substantial town. Prospectors crowded the mountainous Cariboo Wagon Road to seek their fortunes. But few did, and the rush faded. Soon after the rush the present townsite was laid out.

While not a ghost town, Salmo, British Columbia, is a good example of a railway town that has retained its heritage streetscape. The station still stands at the head of the main street.

In 1919, the PGE established a divisional point here, with yards and a two-storey station, similar in style to those that survive in Quesnel and Williams Lake. While the town itself dates from the time of the gold rush, many of the main street buildings, including a pair of hotels, reflect the railway era. Today, a more modern station stands beside the now mostly silent yards, home now to the Kaoham Shuttle service from Lillooet to Seton Portage.

Quesnel, B.C.

The British Columbia Railway was a relative latecomer to British Columbia's mountains, not reaching Prince George until 1952. The original route of the Pacific Great Eastern was only from Squamish to Clinton. The only divisional point on its length, besides Lillooet, was the town of Quesnel, another site of the early gold rush. The PGE halted construction here in 1921 while it figured out a way to conquer the difficult Cottonwood Canyon to the north. Today, Quesnel still contains extensive yards and a two-storey station, much modernized, but little else in the way of railway heritage features. Otherwise, it remains a busy community. An identical station still stands in Williams Lake, although that town never contained divisional facilities.

Salmo, B.C.

Admittedly, Salmo was not a divisional town. But it is one of the West's best preserved examples of a railway town. Along with the rare Great Northern Railway station, built in 1923, sitting at the end of the main street, the town's central artery also features a stunning collection of heritage shops and structures. The streetscape is like a museum piece. Sitting prominently on the corner across from the station is the historic Salmo Hotel, and a string of buildings beside it, including the drug store and liquor store, displaying the Old West boomtown style of storefront, as does the row of wooden stores opposite. Although the trains no longer stop here, the appearance of the village core has changed little since the last train rumbled by the white wooden station on a railway roadbed that is now minus its ties and rails.

THE RAILWAY GHOST TOWNS

Bankhead, AB

Not far from the bustle of Banff and the Banff Springs Hotel, lie the silent ghostly ruins of Bankhead. The town was created in 1904 to supply coal for the CPR steam locomotives. It grew to more than 1,500 residents, many of whom toiled in the dark and noisy underground mines.

At its peak, the town contained more than one hundred homes, plus a hotel, school, stores, and a pool hall, along with a bunkhouse for single men.

But when the mines closed in 1922, the residents moved out, primarily to nearby Banff, and most of the structures were removed, leaving only foundations. Today, Parks Canada has provided pathways and interpretive plaques to guide visitors past the ghosts of this once-vital railway town. A historical exhibit sits in the mine's former transformer station. The Bankhead station, a standard CPR two-storey plan used through the mountains, now serves as a hostel in Banff.

Donald, AB

Donald became a divisional town on the CPR just west of Lake Louise, with station, yards, roundhouse, and a small townsite. It became a ghost town as early as 1897, after the CPR moved the divisional point to Revelstoke. It continued to be an engine water stop and the site of lumber operations, however. Today, no trace remains of the town or the railway facilities, although the Trans-Canada Highway passes over the river on a highway bridge, and the CPR freights rumble right on through.

Dorreen, B.C.

Records do not indicate how large this trackside community became, nor is there a handy town plot. It came to life with the arrival of the Grand Trunk Pacific Railway in 1911 and was named after a GTP engineer named Ernest Dorreen. The station was designed after the standard GTP pattern, with a bell-cast roof and a small dormer above the

Fort Steele, British Columbia, became a ghost town when the CPR bypassed it. It is now a ghost town theme park.

agents' bay window. Today, a smaller boxcar-sized building serves as the rarely used VIA station. But when VIA's *Skeena* train does slow down here, passengers will be able to see the lonely general store, built in 1920, as the sole survivor in an overgrown meadow that marks the townsite.

The store, now a regionally designated heritage site, operated until 1960 and for a few years afterward as a fishing lodge. That's not to say nobody lives there. In recent years, a back-to-the-land movement has brought a group of self-sufficient individuals and families into this remote community. Access remains by train or ATV track.

Fort Steele, B.C.

This "ghost town" began life as a mining boom town, not once but twice. The first gold rush occurred in the 1860s but soon petered out. The second boom came along in 1892 with the discovery of more gold and silver, and the town boomed to more than one thousand residents and eleven hotels. As a proper name for this newly booming town, the townspeople petitioned the government to name their community Fort Steele, to honour RCMP Colonel Sam Steele who had successfully negotiated a peaceful solution to disputes involving the local First Nations band.

Despite the success of the second mining boom, to the dismay of the townspeople the CPR southern main line bypassed the town, choosing instead Cranbrook for its regional headquarters, and soon Fort Steele began to resemble a ghost town. Yet it retained a treasure trove of early historic structure and in 1961 the province declared the town a heritage site. New buildings now intersperse with the old structures, some of which remain ghostly vacant. A tour train operates from a purpose made station. Unfortunately, the original CPR station no longer exists.

Freeport, B.C.

About twenty-four kilometres east of Burns Lake, along the tracks of the GTP, sits a lonely gravestone surrounded by a picket fence. It marks the former railway village of Freeport. The grave is that of one Ed Kelly, who was shot to death by one Jerry Mulvinhill for cheating at cards. When the town later became a ghost town, the property was purchased by Kelly's sister, who burned the remaining buildings to the ground. The site, which includes a railway boxcar (the old station perhaps?), can be viewed from the window of VIA Rail's *Skeena*.

Illecillewaet, B.C.

The site lies about eight kilometres upstream from the Illecillewaet lookout of the Trans-Canada Highway. This now-empty place began life in 1885 as a construction camp for the CPR crews struggling to breach the Rogers Pass. The site grew, serving as a base for an assortment of navvies along with various prospectors and lumbermen. Most of the wooden shacks were constructed with little heed paid to the town plan showing streets and lot lines.

Michel and Natal, B.C.

Thanks to the plentiful coal deposits along the CPR's southern main line in the Crowsnest Valley, a string of towns grew to supply coal to the CPR and coke to Canada's growing mining industry. While a few communities cling to life there still, such as Coleman and Blairmore, others have vanished from the landscape. Natal, Michel, and a smaller community between the two appropriately named Middletown are among them.

A devastating rock slide killed many residents in the railway and coal-mining town of Frank (see page 102).

Many towns once dependent upon the railways and coal mining have become ghost towns, such as Michel in southern B.C.'s coal country. This structure has since been removed.

In 1899, the Crowsnest Coal Company established the mine at Michel, and by 1901, five hundred residents lived in the line of company houses. With the growing demand for coal, the population boomed to 1,200 by 1907. In that year, the company laid out the townsite of Natal, which contained four hotels and a theatre. Here, too, were the mine buildings and the coke ovens, which covered the area with layers of coal dust.

The danger of exploding coal dust took a toll over the years — among other things there was an explosion ignited by lightning that killed three miners.

The grim conditions moved the provincial government to create a new community at Sparwood, and most of the displaced residents relocated there. While a few lonely structures survived after the move, nothing remains at either community to recall the grimy days when Michel and Natal were among the CPR's most important coal towns. The Michel hotel was the last to go, being demolished in 2010.

The townsites lie on Highway 3 in the Crowsnest Pass just west of the Alberta-B.C. border.

Pacific, B.C.

The stone foundations of the railway roundhouse here are the only remnant of what was a strategic divisional point on the route of the Grand Trunk Pacific Railway from Jasper to Prince Rupert. It contained at its peak the roundhouse, a substantial station, a coaling dock, a water tower, and facilities for the crew. The town did not grow much beyond its railway role. The first station burned in the early 1930s and was replaced with a smaller and simpler structure. More than a dozen families occupied the surrounding area, which was considered to have mining potential.

The community began as a steamer landing on the Skeena River about 150 kilometres east of Prince Rupert. Originally named Nicholl, the GTP changed it to Pacific to reflect the rail line's destination. The GTP erected a standard station in 1913 and a twelve-stall roundhouse two years later. The roundhouse was demolished in 1959 when the CN moved its divisional point to Terrace.

Whiley's Directory of British Columbia for 1918 lists James Anderson as the proprietor of the Nichol Hotel, while Haydon and McCubbin operated a store and acted as postmasters and mining recorders. It listed the population as fifty, most of whom were miners. By 1922, it had added Barker's restaurant and a prospectors association as well as the BC Exploration Company. In 1929, the directory was listing fourteen CN employees, the CN News Restaurant, and a school. The last recorded entry in the directory was in 1948, when the population was listed at sixty-four and appeared to include a pool room, Johnstone's mill, a B.C. government ferry service, and even an interior decorator.

The last resident died in 1972. In 1977, the *Victoria Daily Times* reported that the seventy-three lots and eleven remaining houses, plus the community hall, had been bought by a ghost town aficionado with the intent of turning it into a self-sustaining community. Nothing appeared to come of this initiative, and the place remains a silent ghostly relic of the railway era. Pacific is listed as a regional heritage site.

Rogers Pass, B.C.

For the weary workers building the CPR and pushing its tracks over the Rogers Pass, the railway established a construction camp and townsite called Rogers Pass. The location contained a station, roundhouse, and bank. But it was a doomed townsite. In 1899, an avalanche swept through the community, wiping out most of the structures and killing eight. Another deadly slide swept through a decade later. The town managed to struggle on until the Connaught Tunnel opened in 1916, obviating the need for the railway location. Today, the site lies within Rogers Pass National Historic Site, which maintains a park trail to the vanished townsite.

Sandon, B.C.

This booming silver town was served by not just one but two rail lines, the Great Northern's Kaslo and Slocan Railway, and the CPR's Nakusp and Slocan Railway. By the 1890s, Sandon could boast of twenty-four hotels, twenty-three saloons, theatres, opera houses, not to mention its fair share of bordellos, as well as mining offices, general stores and two railway stations. However, the silver ran out and in 1955 a flash flood raced down the narrow valley, sweeping away many of the stores and leaving the rest in a state of ruin.

The construction of a new highway, the end of passenger rail service, and other aspects of railway modernization all combined to bring an end to the railway era in Yahk, British Columbia, which turned it into a photogenic ghost town.

Over the succeeding years, it has come back to life as one of British Columbia's more popular ghost town attractions, with the Sandon Historical Society and Visitor Centre housed in the restored Mercantile Block. In the centre of the ghost town sits a 0-6-0 steam engine (#6947), with a string of freight cars awaiting restoration.

Access to the weathered ruins is along Sandon Road which follows the old railway roadbed from Highway 31A. Idaho Peak Road leads from the main portion of the ghost town to a few more scattered cabins, the railway display and the former K&S railway station.

Walhachin, B.C.

More a rural settlement than a town, Walhachin grew along the Thompson River beside the CPR and CNoR lines about fifty-two kilometres west of Kamloops. The village contained two stations, a water tank, and railway wye, and prospered until the First World War, when the entire male population left to fight overseas. With the male population away, the maintenance of the system of flumes needed to keep the farms going in what is one of Canada's driest regions, failed following a series of torrential storms that washed out the flumes, and the place never recovered.

It was located on the south bank of the Thompson River. Today a handful of village homes lie scattered along the Walhachin Road amid dry grasslands and shrub, while trains rumble by in the distance.

Yahk, B.C.

The population of this community on the Moyie River today numbers about 140, down drastically from the three thousand it had when the construction of the CPR's southern main line was in full swing. The two-storey station built there lasted from 1912 until 1982, while the yards once contained a wye, a coal chute, and a water tower. The businesses lined the main street behind the station. Today, no station survives and the silent main street consists of a pair of former hotels, one abandoned and the other converted to apartments. A few homes and businesses lie on Highway 3 nearby. The community lies between Cranbrook and Creston.

Ymir, B.C.

Ymir owes its origins not to the railway but to the nearby gold mines, once the most extensive in the world. The tracks of the Great Northern Railway came through in 1897, and the railway added a siding, a station, and a water tower. Today the railway roadbed forms part of a rail trail, while the grid network of streets contain only a few dwellings. Near the old rail line, the historic Ymir Hotel continues to serve refreshments, while a heritage fire hall now sits nearby. Ymir lies a short distance off Highway 6 between Salmo and Nelson.

TOWN NAMES

Besides the usual tendency to name stations after railway brass, Andrew McCulloch decided to open up his Shakespeare and name a string of stations between Brookmere and Hope after his favourite Shakespearean characters. And so in order we find Juliet, Romeo, Iago (from *Othello*), Portia (*Merchant of Venice*), Aurum (originally Venice), Jessica (from *Merchant of Venice*), Lear, and Othello.

THE DREAM CASTLES: WESTERN CANADA'S RAILWAY HOTELS

Railway hotels, for the most part, served the basic needs of the rail traveller. Most were simple two- or three-storey structures, built of wood or brick, located close to the station. Urban stations naturally required grander hotels. The Nova Scotian in Halifax, the Royal York in Toronto, and the Chateau Laurier in Ottawa all reflect the grand urban design that the railways used to attract the travelling public. The Fort Garry in Winnipeg, the Bessborough in Saskatoon, and the Palliser in Calgary also survive to remind us of the railways' hotel-building legacy.

The railways were not blind to the tourist potential of other areas through which they passed either. The chateau-style Algonquin Resort in New Brunswick, the Chateau Montebello near Gatineau, and the world famous Chateau Frontenac in Quebec City all testify to that vision. In fact, six of Canada's grandest railway hotels are now National Historic Sites.

But few regions in Canada could rival the stunning scenery of Canada's western mountains, especially the Rockies. And it was here that the irascible CPR president William Cornelius Van Horne declared that if he couldn't bring the scenery to the tourists he would bring the tourists to the scenery. And so the CPR went from being the national political unifier to being an international tourist attraction.

THE DREAM CASTLES

The earliest of the CPR's "dream castles," as Van Horne liked to describe them, began life as key dining stations. As the early locomotives lacked the power to haul the heavy dining cars up the steep mountain grades, the CPR built stations in which to accommodate the hungry travellers. Among these were the Fraser Canyon House, the Mount Stephen House, and the Glacier House. The stunning scenery that surrounded them drew travellers back for longer stays, often involving hiking and skiing, and so the CPR continuously added on to them. All were similar in style, using a plan devised by architect Thomas Sorby and stood three stories high with two-storey wings. Their days declined when gentler grades on the lines and heavier loco-motives eliminated the need to stop for meals and hotels were reduced to crew bunkhouses or were bypassed by straighter tracks. All languished and eventually came down.

Glacier House

Opened in 1887, Glacier House, which was located at the foot of the Illecillewaet Glacier, soon began to attract alpinists from Europe to the "Canadian Alps," as the railway promoted them. In 1890, the hotel doubled in size from fifteen to thirty-two rooms. But after the railway rerouted its line from the steep grades to the more distant Connaught Tunnel, Glacier House became less accessible. It closed in 1925 and was demolished four years later. Its ruins lie along a trail managed by Parks Canada in Rogers Pass National Historic Site. From the Illecillewaet campground, a short trail leads to an exhibit at the site of the grand old hotel.

Mount Stephen House

Located in the Kicking Horse Valley in the divisional town of Field, the Mount Stephen House opened in 1886 with a mere fifteen rooms, but by 1902 had been enlarged to more than one hundred guest rooms, all with private baths, still a novelty at the time. To further attract tourists to the region, the CPR added lodges at Lake O'Hara, Emerald Lake, and Wapta Lake in the Yoho Valley. By 1909, the opening of the Spiral Tunnels had obviated the need for the location as a dining station, and in 1918 the hotel was transferred to the YMCA for use as a railway hotel for the train crews, a role it played

until 1963 when the railway YMCA division was winding down, and the structure was demolished.

Fraser Canyon House

Built in the CPR divisional town of North Bend on the Fraser River, Fraser Canyon House opened in 1887, and expanded ten years later; however, it lacked the alpine appeal of the others. It burned in 1927 and was replaced by a new structure that was used by the CPR crews into the 1970s. This was ultimately replaced by a more modern bunk house. A second hotel, the Mount View Hotel, stood behind the CPR hotel but was vacant by the 1980s and no longer stands.

Banff Springs Hotel

Van Horne envisioned something bigger than the modest dining station/hotels the CPR initially built. And so in 1893 he embarked upon the construction of what is still considered Canada's grandest resort hotel, the Banff Springs Hotel, now a Fairmont property.

The development of Banff really all began with a chance discovery, when Franklin McCabe, and William and Thomas McCardell discovered a mineral hot springs in the area of what is now Banff, Alberta, in 1885. Anticipating that a profit could be made from the promotion of the spring as a spa, they built a cabin to establish a land claim. Despite their dream to profit from their squatters' rights, the trio instead accepted $675 each from the CPR president William Cornelius Van Horne for rights to the land. Unknown to the three individuals, Van Horne had estimated the

The construction of the Banff Springs Hotel marked the beginning of the CPR's major venture into tourism and launched the tourism era in the mountains of southern Alberta and British Columbia.

springs were worth a million dollars for a potential hotel development.

Van Horne then lobbied the federal government to declare the whole area a protected natural area — to enhance the natural appeal of the mountains and to increase the investment potential of his hotel as well. The government designated the region as one of Canada's first national parks and gave Van Horne the go-ahead to construct one of Canada's most spectacular hotels: the Banff Springs Hotel.

Van Horne selected his star architect, Bruce Price, to create a chateau-style resort. The site selected for the hotel was a hilltop with a stunning view down the canyon of the Bow River. But when the contractor had finished, Van Horne discovered that the hotel faced the wrong way. The best views belonged not to the paying guests but, instead, to the chefs in the kitchen. Van Horne remedied that problem in short order by tacking on a rotunda in front of the kitchen.

The spectacular view along the valley of the Bow River continues to attract visitors to the Fairmont Banff Springs Hotel.

The five-storey wooden chateau was able to accommodate 280 guests when it opened in 1888. Despite the attraction of skiing and other winter activities in the area, for several years the hotel remained a summer-only operation. The guests, who were transported from the simple log train station to the hotel in a carriage pulled by a team of groomed horses, were offered the opportunity to enjoy canoeing on the Bow River, Swiss-led guided treks up the mountains, golfing on the golf course, or, of course, a dip in the hot springs.

By the turn of the century, Van Horne's boast that it would be the grandest hotel in the continent was close to being fulfilled when Baedeker's Guide rated it among Canada's top five hotels, and within a few years was considered among North America's top three.

But the chateau was quickly becoming too popular for the arriving tourists, many of whom had to sleep in the station itself. And so, in 1911, architect Walter S. Painter began work on a new chateau. Rundlestone, a stone that has the amazing ability to change colour from blue to brown after exposure to the sun, was hauled in to build the eleven-storey central tower.

By 1914, the new chateau was ready to receive its guests, among whom were the Duke and Duchess of Connaught and U.S. president Teddy Roosevelt. Two new additions to the hotel opened in 1925 and 1926. Sadly, however, in March of 1926 fire completely destroyed what was left of the original wooden hotel.

Over the years since, the hotel has continued to attract royalty, politicians, and the Hollywood glitterati. In 1969, the hotel finally opened for the winter season, becoming an all-seasons resort.

Much has been preserved of the hotel and much added. While a new guest entrance has now opened, the original lobby has been preserved as the Rundle Hall. The original 1928 Mount Stephen Hall hosts elegant dining and special events. Heritage Hall, located upstairs from the main lobby, displays historic photos depicting the story of the hotel and its builders. Today, more than one thousand staff tend to the upwards of one thousand guests who stay in 778 guest rooms, while ten restaurants, bars, and grills provide sustenance. The exterior offers four stunning terraces from which to view the mountain scenery while a statue of William Cornelius Van Horne greets arriving visitors in the driveway.

Despite strict planning controls in the federal townsite, Banff is bursting at the seams with tour buses, condos, and high-end shops. About the only thing that is missing is the thing that started it all in the first place: the trains. No regular passenger train has called since the rerouting of VIA Rail in 1990. Only the luxurious tour train, the *Rocky Mountaineer*, comes this way and maintains a ticket counter in the station. The station now houses a café and bus depot and is rarely visited by the hordes of visitors.

Chateau Lake Louise

Unlike the Banff Springs Hotel, the grand hotel at Lake Louise had humble beginnings. In fact, it literally began as a fishing shack, owned by a pair of CPR employees at the end of a rough trail from Laggan station. However, it soon began to attract day-trippers from Banff, and Van Horne ordered the construction of a dining chalet to accommodate them. When that burned in 1893, a new two-storey log chalet was built to replace it. Van Horne dubbed it the "hotel for the outdoor adventurer and alpinist." In fact, it became known as the birthplace of Canadian mountaineering. From 1890 to 1912 it went from hosting fifty guests to ten thousand.

As Lake Louise's reputation as an alpinist's haven grew, more additions appeared, including a concrete wing designed by the Banff Springs' Walter Painter. When the old wooden portion burned in 1924, a new nine-storey tower appeared in its place. Swiss guides led famous visitors into the snow-covered peaks, among them Douglas Fairbanks, Mary Astor, and John Barrymore, as well as director Alfred Hitchcock and Marilyn Monroe and "the latest celebs whose privacy (the hotel) would like to protect." Films featuring the lake and mountains have included *Eternal Love* (1929), *Springtime in the Rockies* (1942), and *Son of Lassie* (1945).

Travellers arriving at the elegant log station would climb onto a tram to make the journey up the steep road to the shores of the lake. By 1974, the growing popularity of skiing had changed the operation into a year-round resort facility. In 1979 it closed for renovations, reopening in 1988 to host among other events the Lake Louise World Cup of skiing.

The Chateau Lake Louise was built a short distance from the grand hotel in Banff.

Today, guides once more lead guests into the spectacular mountain peaks. With the opening of the Trans-Canada Highway, the stunning lake now attracts hordes of day visitors, including weekend visitors from nearby Calgary as well as lines of large tour buses.

Many of its early architectural features remain, including the stunning Victoria Ballroom in the Painter Wing and the main lobby entrance. The view from the Lakeview Lounge restaurant and from the trails that lead along the shoreline is breathtaking, featuring the high, snow-capped peaks reflected in the blue-green, glacier-fed waters. The view is one of the most photographed in the Rockies.

But Chateau Lake Louise is not the area's only rail-related heritage building. Located beside the free public parking lot by the lake (located a short distance from the hotel's own guest parking lot) stands Deer Lodge, a wide-roofed, rustic wooden building. This was added in 1920 by the CPR to accommodate the Swiss

The view from the Chateau Lake Louise across the lake offers one of the Rocky Mountains' most stunning views.

mountain guides employed by the railway. A wonderfully rustic part-log building, it opened to the public in 1921 when the Trans-Canada Highway was extended from Banff to Lake Louise.

Jasper Park Lodge

Like Van Horne decades earlier, the CNR's first president, Henry Thornton, felt that the remarkable scenery that surrounded the CN's mountain stations was worth exploiting. Looking for an ideal site, Thornton came upon a collection of tents on the shores of Lac Beauvert. One of his first forays into the recreation field was to buy what was called Tent City and replace the canvas dwellings with new log cabins. He called the new development the Jasper Park Lodge. He then ordered the CNR's chief architects, John Schofield and Godfrey Milnes, to redesign the facility.

In 1923, using peeled logs and fieldstone, they created what was at the time the world's largest single-storey log structure. Around it stood a village of bungalow cabins, which ranged from four to twenty rooms. Beside it they laid what remains one of the world's most scenic golf courses. But the links attracted more than their share of local wildlife and one unfortunate golfer watched as his golf ball disappeared in the jaws of a bear. The establishment of Jasper National Park helped to preserve the natural beauty which surrounded the lodge, and the surrounding area retains its great scenic beauty today.

Sadly, in 1952, a fire that broke out in the cloakroom completely destroyed the historic main lodge. A year later, however, a new building stood in its place. Following that sad lesson, many of the old cabins were replaced with fire resistant cedar structures. Today the lodge boasts 111 buildings and twenty-two kilometres of walkways.

Not too surprisingly the lodge and the beauty of the park has attracted the attention of Hollywood. Film crews showed up to create movies such as *The Country Beyond* (1926), *The Emperor Waltz* (1948), *The Far Country* (1954), and the haunting *River of No Return* (1954), which starred Marilyn Monroe and Robert Mitchum. Over the years, the lodge has attracted both royalty and a bevy of celebrity visitors as well, including King George VI and Queen Elizabeth, Bing Crosby for the golf, and Pierre Trudeau.

Jasper National Park is a UNESCO World Heritage Site and attracts many visitors, although they seldom arrive by train anymore.

Hotel Vancouver

When the CPR's new western terminal of Port Moody proved to have an inadequate harbour, Van Horne pushed his line through to the village of Granville, which had grown around Gassy Jack's raucous shanty town known to this day as Gastown. A year after engine #647 pulled the first transcontinental passenger train into the newly named Vancouver, Van Horne began work on a new hotel, the Hotel Vancouver. Several blocks from the CPR station, the first version of the brick hotel stood a mere five stories tall and soon proved inadequate. Staff had to haul water to individual rooms by bucket and the plaster soon began tumbling from the ceilings. Bricks were crumbling and rats and cockroaches ran amok.

By 1916, architects Thomas Sorby and Francis Rattenbury had created a new, fifteen-storey hotel, with arched entrances and bay windows that extended to the top floor. Besides being a railway hotel, it quickly became Vancouver's social centre and arguably its grandest building.

Soon after, the Canadian National Railways began work on its own hotel, the British Columbian. But instead of competing with each other, the two railways joined ranks and both moved into the CNR hotel, adopting the name Hotel Vancouver which opened in 1939. Ten years later, Eaton's purchased the older hotel and demolished it for a parking lot. Among the new hotel's first visitors were King George VI and Queen Elizabeth, who stayed there while on their famous 1939 cross-country tour to raise funds for war bonds.

Designed by the CNR architect John Schofield, the new hotel stood seventeen stories and was topped by a steep, green-copper roof, somewhat reminiscent of the Chateau Laurier in Ottawa.

While neither old — it was built in the 1930s — nor near a rail line, the Hotel Vancouver is nonetheless one of the West's finer railway hotels.

Modernization in the 1960s destroyed many of the building's original features. Happily, restorations in 1986 and 1996 restored much of the hotel's historic aura, with new fixtures and décor reflecting its railway roots, although few guests arrive by train these days. Today, the hotel is a protected heritage building. It is located on West Georgia Street.

Near the VIA station on Main Street, the Ivanhoe Hotel, built in 1907, is the last survivor of a string of hotels, which included the Cobalt and the American hotels, to serve travellers arriving on the GNR and the CNR railways.

Empress Hotel

Although it was built by the hotel-crazed CPR, Victoria's Empress Hotel could not really be called a "railway" hotel, since Victoria at the time had no railways. Rather, it served well-heeled travellers arriving on the CPR's luxury ocean liners. Designed by CPR architect Frances Rattenbury, the chateau-style brick beauty opened in 1908, providing arriving ocean travellers with a spectacular view from the ships' decks. The luxury of the plush cream-and-red interiors matched the style of the vessels themselves. Additions were made to the hotel in 1910 and 1929. Teas took place in the Lounge (and still do), while guests danced the night away in the Crystal Ballroom.

Despite the glory of the hotel, the CPR pretty much left the building on its own and it showed. By 1954, even the wiring was outdated. The CPR quietly considered tearing down the hotel, but the possibility of demolishing Victoria's grandest building so outraged the residents that the CPR quickly scrapped the notion. Instead, in 1988 it added a new wing and undertook a $45 million renovation to restore the hotel's original elegance. The Crystal Ballroom, the Gold Lounge and Empress Room all reflect that heritage. Still a magnet for the rich and famous — the hotel has hosted everyone from Douglas Fairbanks Jr. to Harrison Ford — The Empress remains one of the city's most loved and visited tourist attractions.

The Janion

Built in 1891, the Janion, with forty-eight guest rooms, served as one of Victoria's first major hotels. It stands adjacent to the location of Victoria's first E&N station and for a time contained that railway's offices. It was known at the time as a credible and commodious hotel, with twenty-five cent dinners and — typical for the period when it opened — "white cooks" only. As a temperance hotel — a hotel without a liquor license — it suffered financially and eventually went out of business. In subsequent years it served variously as a warehouse, an assayer's office, the offices for the railway, and, briefly, as a bottling plant for Pacific Beer. In 2008, in order to prevent its demolition, the city declared the dilapidated former hotel a heritage structure. That effort paid off — in 2015 it was undergoing a $2.5 million refit to accommodate one hundred micro lofts.

The Swans

The Swans Hotel, across from the site of Victoria's former CPR station, began life in 1913 as a granary and warehouse. The grain trains would enter into the building through what is today the hotel's main entrance. In the 1950s it became Buckfield's feed store. Then, in the 1980s, a visionary named Michael Williams acquired a number of heritage properties on Lower Johnson Street, the heart of historic Victoria, with the intention of repurposing them and preserving their heritage character. In 1989, the old feed store became the Swans Hotel, with twenty-nine boutique hotel rooms and an award winning three-thousand-square-foot penthouse. It also contains a brewpub and is a focus for the arts community in Victoria.

On the opposite corner, the former Station Hotel now serves as the Goodfellas Cigar Shop, and a block away along Johnson Avenue at Store Street, the attractive three-storey former Grand Pacific Hotel (not to be confused with a new Grand Pacific hotel, which recently opened) now contains a string of shops, including a Famosa Restaurant. The former identity of the building lives on, however, in the name that lingers on the upper wall of the building.

THE LOCAL RAILWAY HOTELS

Along the tracks, both those now gone and those that still remain, many small railway towns yet retain their early hotel buildings. Among the more charming are the Greenwood Hotel, the Coalmont Hotel, the two one-time Yahk hotels — neither of which are still in operation, the rustic hotel at Ymir, and the fine-looking Salmo Hotel. The old railway hotel in the former divisional town of Endako continues to function as a drinking establishment. All stood across the road opposite the former station grounds and offered rest and respite for train travellers.

The Occidental

This two-storey Italianate hotel was built in Nanaimo in 1887 to accommodate passengers arriving on the newly opened E&N Railway linking Victoria with Courtenay along the coast of Vancouver Island. Its style incorporates arched windows and raised parapets. Located close to the station, which became a restaurant after its restoration, the hotel serves as the entrance from the station to Nanaimo's main street. Listed on the Canadian Register of Historic Places, it sits on the corner of Fitzwilliam and Selby streets.

The Quilchena Hotel

This fine building began as a railway hotel for a railway that never arrived. When the CPR indicated that it would create a divisional point at Nicola on the KVR, Joseph Guichon, a rancher, built a stunning three-storey hotel, the Quilchena Hotel. The railway instead decided to run the tracks along the Coldwater Valley to Merritt, where the coal mines held greater promise for the railway. The stunning wooden structure rises two and a half stories and is topped with a bell-cast roof. Above the porch, with its four wooden pillars, is an enclosed balcony. After closing in 1917, the hotel reopened in 1957, and now operates as a boutique hotel, with fifteen rooms, a restaurant, and a bar and grill. It is located a short distance north of Merritt.

The Yale

The Yale Hotel in Vancouver was built in 1889 as the Colonial Hotel in the heart of Yaletown, to house CPR workers and train travellers. It stands three stories high, with five arched windows on the second-floor sides and peaked dormers in the third-storey mansard roof. In later years, it became a popular jazz club and has recently been renovated. It is situated at 1300 Granville Street.

The Railway Club

Situated closer to Vancouver's historic CPR station than The Yale, the Railway Club opened in 1931 to cater to CPR station employees. With its dark wood interior and period chandeliers, the Railway Club has retained much of that 1930s' ambience, although the shops at street level display typical modern facades. It is situated upstairs at the intersection of Dunsmuir and Seymour streets, about six blocks from the CPR station. The toy train that circles the ceiling may be a more recent addition.

THE DISAPPEARED

Sadly, many hotels, grand in their time, outlived their purpose and have gone.

Cameron Lake Chalet Resort

Built in 1912 by the CPR, the Cameron Lake Chalet Resort (not to be confused with the currently existing Cameron Lake Resort) similarly served as a station/hotel and stood on the CPR branch line to Port Alberni. It overlooked the shores of Cameron Lake, and was built in a Swiss-chalet style, with a second-floor, half-timber cross gable. In 1915 it was leased out and provided continuous service as a resort until 1966. It has since been removed. The site lies at the end of Chalet Road a short distance north of Highway 4.

Rainbow Lodge

Some may find it hard to believe that the world-renowned Whistler Resort complex began as a simple railway lodge. When the Pacific Great Eastern Railway (later BC Rail) opened its line from the ocean port of Squamish to Clinton, it recognized the tourist potential of the scenery and lakes through which it passed. Built on the northwest shore of Alta Lake by Alex and Myrtle Philip the year before the tracks arrived, their simple log chalet, called the Rainbow

Lodge, became a popular destination for rail passengers, hunters, and fishers. Alex Philip, who was also a fiction writer, nicknamed such local landmarks as the "Bridge of Sighs" and the "River of Golden Dreams."

By the 1940s, the lodge could offer more than one hundred rooms. It operated until 1977 when sadly the main lodge burned. In recognition of the heritage of this railway hotel, the name lives on in Rainbow Park on Alta Lake Road, which contains some of the surviving cabins from the lodge, and a replica of the "Bridge of Sighs."

After 1965, when the B.C. government opened the first road link to the area, Whistler began to develop as a major ski destination. In 1977, the concept of a ski resort village began to take shape. By 1992, *Snow Country* magazine was voting the resort North America's number one ski resort. In 2003 it won the bid to host the 2010 Winter Olympics, along with the City of Vancouver. With the upgrading of the Sea to Sky Highway for the Olympics, Whistler has become today a sprawling maze of condos, chalets, hotels, and shops.

During that period the trains continued to call at a small station. Today, BC Rail has ended its passenger service, although the *Rocky Mountaineer* maintains a rustic log and stone station in the upscale Nita Lake Lodge on Lake Placid Road.

Sicamous Hotel

The Sicamous Hotel, a combined station/hotel erected in 1897 by the CPR, overlooked the waters of Shuswap Lake. It became a popular tourist destination when it was rebuilt in 1900 after fire destroyed the first structure. It served as a stop on the transcontinental line and a transfer point for travellers connecting to Vernon. Following extensive renovations, it continued to lure travellers until the CPR closed it in 1956. It stood until 1964 when it was demolished. The hostelry contained seventy-five rooms as well as a large popular dining hall and ballroom.

Strathcona Hotel

The Strathcona Hotel on Shawnigan Lake on Vancouver Island, rebuilt after a fire in 1900, opened as a hotel alone until 1916, when the CPR acquired it and operated it as a hotel/station, offering thirty-two rooms as well as a tennis court and croquet lawn. The CPR sold the building and it became a girls' school in 1927, although it continued to function as a stop for the E&N. It was demolished in 1969.

Other grand plans never realized the light of day, such as the Grand Trunk Pacific Hotel in Prince Rupert, the GTP's Chateau Mount Robson near the Alberta border, the Grand Trunk Pacific Hotel in Victoria (although the GTP came nowhere near Victoria), or the GTP's Chateau Miette in Jasper, intended as a rival for the CPR's Banff Springs Hotel.

RAILWAY STRUCTURES: A FORGOTTEN HERITAGE

Clearly, the key heritage structure for the railways was the railway station. But during the heyday of rail travel, many structures were in place to help operate the mighty steam engines. These included water towers, made mostly of steel but many of wood; the all-important roundhouses and turntables, where steam engines were shuttled for maintenance; and freight sheds, telegraph offices, and ticket offices — all vital elements in rail operation. Section houses provided accommodation for the line men, while bunkhouses were vital to divisional points, providing shelter for the train crews to rest between shifts. Many such locations also included individual housing for more senior management, and there was even more elaborate housing for executives.

As important as all of these structures once were, most have now vanished from the landscape — longer trains now bypass the divisional points, diesel replaced the need for water towers and coal docks, while computerized traffic control and the demise of passenger travel ended many station jobs.

THE ROUNDHOUSES

Every divisional point had a roundhouse, necessary for the maintenance of the large steam locomotives. For the most part, they tended to be located in a remote corner of the rail yard, so as to not impede yard operations. The earliest were built of wood or stone. But with the arrival of larger and heavier locomotives, these early structures were replaced with newer ones, having larger stalls and longer turntables.

Roundhouses originated, as did the railways, in England. The earliest versions, built in the 1820s, were square in shape, with the tracks running directly through them. Later versions had a different design: the engines entered and exited the same entrance. This was a result of the fact that the lines were adding more engines to their fleets, and the engine houses required additional space and greater ease of entering. A solution to the fact that steam locomotives could only go forward was the turntable, on which the engines would sit while the turntable moved the engine to its assigned stall.

Inside, pits beneath the engines allowed for greasing, oiling, and cleaning the flues. Vents in the roof allowed the smoke to escape. With the replacement of steam with diesel, new techniques came into play, and roundhouses were replaced with more modern engine shops. And since diesels could move both forward and backward, turntables were no longer needed. Nor did maintenance need to be done every 150 kilometres, and so the roundhouses came down, replaced in only a few vital locations by more modern engine houses. Of the more than forty roundhouses that once stood in British Columbia and the mountains of Alberta, only six remain, and two of these were created in recent years for railway museums, while another now consists only of foundations. Because of their single-purpose construction and generally remote locations, few presented an opportunity for repurposing and the railway companies felt no compulsion to preserve them. So, sadly, few remain.

Cranbrook CPR Roundhouse

Here, in one of Canada's premier rail towns, lies what may be the last functioning railway-owned roundhouse in Canada's western mountains. The original six stalls were built in 1907, using the CPR engine-house plan #2, and the remaining ten in 1920, according to plan #2A. In 1989, when the CPR had decided that the oldest stalls of its sixteen-stall roundhouse were no longer needed, the City of Cranbrook commissioned the Iredale Group to investigate the possible re-use of this historic site. Although Iredale offered proposals for a museum use, the CPR opposed this due to security and operational concerns.

However, in 2015, the CPR announced that the roundhouse would be retained, including the original six stalls, although some renovations will be undertaken. The CPR yard in Cranbrook is quieter now, with the railway having moved its switching operations to Fort Steele Junction a short distance away. While there is no public access to the roundhouse, it can be seen across the tracks from the rail museum.

Cranbrook CPR Freight Shed

Among the oldest railway structures in this busy railway town is the 1898 CPR freight shed. The five-thousand-square-foot structure was shifted in 1999 onto a new concrete foundation adjacent to the main museum building to provide space for exhibition galleries and two operating model railway displays.

Pacific Roundhouse

In 1915, as the Grand Trunk Pacific Railway was completing its Winnipeg to Prince Rupert railway, it established a vital divisional point on the Skeena River 150 kilometres from Prince Rupert. Here, according to its standard roundhouse plan (120-115), it erected a twelve-stall roundhouse encircling a turntable. The site also included a large station, a water tank, an oil tank, and sanding facilities, in addition to a divisional townsite.

In 1959, when diesel had replaced steam and the CN relocated the divisional point to Terrace, the Pacific roundhouse came down. It is worthy to note that the District of Kitimat-Stikine has declared the foundations to be a regional historical site. The region's heritage

One of the few roundhouses in Canada to remain in use by a railway is that in Cranbrook, British Columbia. It's a structure that the city hopes to retain.

evaluation report identifies the heritage elements as including the form of the remains of the foundations, its townsite's flat terrain, its location near the river, and other on-site remains, as well as its vital role in the opening of the railway and the settlement of the region.

Access to this remote location is challenging, although the roundhouse ruins are visible from the windows of VIA's *Skeena* as it passes.

West Coast Heritage Railway Roundhouse, Squamish, B.C.

While the roundhouse in this large railway museum is not original to the BCR, it was constructed in 2005 to house much of the museum's collection, including the iconic *Royal Hudson* locomotive. An operating turntable sits in front. The roundhouse additionally provides space for conferences and meetings.

The roundhouse in the tourist attraction of Three Valley Gap, situated near Revelstoke, British Columbia, is a modern structure built to house historic railway equipment.

Three Valley Gap Heritage Ghost Town, Revelstoke, B.C.

Touted as housing the largest fully operational covered turntable in North America, the roundhouse in this tourist attraction known as Three Valley Gap Heritage Ghost Town is not an original railway roundhouse. Rather, it was constructed as an operating replica, and is part of the tourist attraction. The lobby of the roundhouse is a replica of the historic Arlington Court building in Revelstoke. The turntable inside measures more than thirty metres and rotates toward the twenty-four bays, which contain a variety of heritage railway rolling stock. The complex also contains a back shop and carpentry and coach repair shop. The site also features a collection of heritage buildings, vintage cars, and a newly opened hotel.

The CPR roundhouse in Vancouver's Yaletown was preserved as part of the City's Expo 86 transportation exposition.

Yaletown Roundhouse, Vancouver, B.C.

In 1887, the newly opened CPR decided to move its repair facilities from Yale in the Fraser Canyon to a more convenient location near its terminus at Vancouver. The most appropriate site lay on the north shore of False Creek, which is where the railway established many of its West Coast facilities. The roundhouse itself was constructed in 1888 as a ten-stall

brick-and-stone structure. In 1911, twelve more bays were added and the existing ones lengthened.

With the advent of dieselization, the roundhouse sat empty, subject to demolition by the federal government. In 1984, the BC Place Corporation acquired the building to form a pavilion for Expo 86, after which the building once more sat empty. But then, in 1993, plans to develop the north side of False Creek happily incorporated the roundhouse as a heritage feature, and in 1994 plans were drawn up to convert the structure into a community arts centre. An adjacent glass pavilion was incorporated to house one of Canada's most historic steam locomotives, #374, which hauled the first transcontinental passenger into Vancouver in 1887. New development has replaced the CPR's Yaletown yards and structures, leaving only the roundhouse and turntable to recall this once vital legacy in Vancouver.

Victoria Roundhouse, Victoria, B.C.

One of Canada's best surviving examples of a roundhouse is that in Esquimalt, now Victoria, B.C. Opened in 1913 on the Esquimalt and Nanaimo Railway, it consists of ten stalls, which face onto a twenty-eight-metre turntable. Located on the site of Victoria's original terminus, namely the former naval base at Esquimalt Harbour opposite the city of Victoria, the complex is the creation of the CPR, which operated the E&N at the time. Despite the advent of diesel, the roundhouse and its affiliated buildings continued in use until the end of train service on the line in 2011. Because it remained in railway use, many interior features are still in place. A machine shop with two arched entranceways stands nearby.

When a leaking roof threatened the structure, the city took the CPR to court to force the company to repair it. The CPR countered with the argument that, as a federally charted railway, it was not subject to the city's bylaws and regulations. However, the railway opted to settle out of court and agreed to the repairs.

Due to the many related on-site structures, including the turntable, sidings, car shop, and stores building, its age, and the role it played in the evolution of railways on Vancouver Island, the site became a National Historic Site in 1992. The site is now part of a development proposal for the area. It will be known as Roundhouse Plaza and will form a community focus for a residential development known as Bayview Place.

WATER TOWERS

These vital structures appeared at roughly every other station to provide water to the thirsty steam engines. Large tanks sat inside the skin of these structures, which was constructed of either wood, as was the case in the earlier versions, or steel. The tanks in the towers held the water necessary to replenish the tanks of the steam locomotives, which, in turn, supplied the water for the boilers. It was the boilers that provided the steam that drove the pistons on the large wheels. In the wooden towers, a ball that sat on a floating rod above the tank indicated the water level inside. Pumps inside the tanks would keep the water from freezing, a threat in the frigid mountains of the West. With dieselization, the need for water towers ended and, so, these have almost utterly vanished from the railway landscapes. The few that remain are being preserved for their heritage value.

The CPR's former Esquimalt, British Columbia, roundhouse, Canada's oldest, is a National Historic Site and set to be part of a large scale residential and commercial development.

Brookmere, B.C.

The little Kettle Valley Railway divisional town of Brookmere is but a ghost of its former self. Here two railway lines, the KVR and the Great Northern Railway, shared trackage rights. While the town once contained a large station, a roundhouse, yards, and a section house, little remains. However, one of those features is the unusual two-sided water tower, moved a short distance off its original foundation. The rare twin spouts allowed for the watering of engines on the two rail lines. The tracks of the respective lines also passed on opposite sides of the station. The station name board decorates the side of the old section foreman's house. The tracks are gone and the roadbed has become part of the Kettle Valley Rail Trail.

Water towers usually have little repurposing potential except as historic features. This tower in Cranbrook, British Columbia, is part of the railway museum.

Cranbrook, B.C.

The rare wooden water tower in Cranbrook was built in 1946 to replace an earlier structure. Its twelve-thousand-gallon tank remains inside the wooden shell, which is built of wooden staves held together by steel rods. Now forming part of the Cranbrook Railway Heritage Area, this wooden CPR water tower was moved from its original site onto a

new foundation in 1995. The tower rises more than eight metres above the adjacent tracks.

Field, B.C.

Almost as rare as the wooden water tower in Cranbrook is the steel water tower in Field. This kind of tower, once ubiquitous across the country, was erected in 1930 to

Few railway water towers have survived the dieselization of the railways. This one, in Field, British Columbia, is one of many historic railway structures in that community to survive.

Lone Butte, B.C.

Before it halted construction at the Cottonwood Canyon north of Quesnel, the Pacific Great Eastern Railway had reached the community of Lone Butte, which, prior to the arrival of the rail line, was the centre of cattle ranches and a gold rush. In 1919, the PGE established a construction camp there, and the following year George Duncan McFee and Lee Brown laid out a 122-lot townsite. Lone Butte was a station and water tower location. Even though the station is gone, the 1920 water tower remains, preserved now by the Lone Butte Historical Association. Painted in green, and fully sheathed in wooden staves, it stands in a park at the east end of the village on Highway 24 close to its original track side location.

Parksville, B.C.

Built with the arrival of the E&N railway running from Victoria to Courtenay on Vancouver Island in 1911, Parksville's wooden water tower, with its timber foundations, survived dieselization only to be threatened with demolition in the 1990s. When the occupants of the station and the town realized the demise of the historic tower was imminent, they rallied support to save it. Following a fundraising drive, the tower was relocated off railway property and onto an adjacent municipal parkette.

Port Alberni, B.C.

Similar in style to the one in Parksville, the E&N water tower in Port Alberni is located adjacent to the station. The wooden tower, which dates from 1912, consists of

replace a wooden structure. With the arrival of dieselization it the 1950s, it was retired from service, but it still stands proudly in this historic railway divisional town, rising twenty-one metres above the rail yards. Field also has retained a rare surviving CPR telegraph house. Added in the 1920s, its brick facade and windows remain intact.

a wooden tank with wooden beams providing support at the base. Although the Port Alberni steam train operation requires a water supply, the tank itself is no longer used. The base has been rebuilt and the tank restored.

OTHER STRUCTURES

Beehive Coke Ovens, Crowsnest Pass, AB

The hills of southwestern Alberta, and the Crowsnest Pass in particular, held major deposits of coal, which was vital to the operation of steam locomotives and to Canada's industries. With the arrival of the CPR and the Great Northern Railway into the region in 1909, the Crowsnest came alive with coal mining towns, most of which were later abandoned. Coleman, Blairmore, and Bellevue are but a few of those which still survive. Many were company towns, like Michel, Natal, and Passmore, which were simply dismantled or demolished when the coal era ended.

Coke is made by burning coal in large brick ovens and is used in the processing of metal ores. More than 1,700 such ovens lined the tracks in these smoky places, most of which operated between 1903 and 1918. Out of a total of 216 in the Crowsnest Pass, 104 were reactivated in the years between 1932 and 1952. Of these, 68 remain, including those in Coleman.

The nearby Leitch Collieries Provincial Historic Site, which, like the others in the Pass, was serviced by the CPR, offers tours of the Roman-like ruins of the coal-processing plant, including its coke ovens. These collieries, which lasted only from 1911 until 1915, were the only Canadian-owned and operated plant in the Crowsnest Pass. The site contains, in addition to the plant, the former manager's house, a coal tipple and a row of coking ovens, thirty-two of which had never been fired before the mines closed. A workers' town known as Passburg was built west of the site, but, like most of the others in the Pass, was dismantled when the mine closed and has left no visible remains.

The Pass is more tragically noted for the deadly Frank slide. On April 28 of 1903, the entire side of Turtle Mountain broke loose and roared down upon the town of Frank, crushing seventy-six victims to death. The massive blocks are spread throughout the area and remain a frightful sight to this day. A nearby interpretive centre recalls that fateful day.

Coal Shed, Summerland, B.C.

Like water towers and roundhouses, coal docks and sheds have disappeared from the railway landscapes. For nearly its entire length, the route of the Kettle Valley Railway is now a rail trail. But north of Summerland the tracks remain in place and host the popular steam excursions of the Kettle Valley Steam Railway. While the train operates from a new purpose-built station, the handsome wooden station that stood in the nearby town of Summerland has gone. Opposite the location of the station however remains the derelict shell of the former coal shed.

CNR Engine House, Prince Rupert, B.C.

Within view of the Kwinitsa station museum, the old, red wooden, two-stall CNR engine house still stands,

Coal was vital to Canada's early railways and industries. These coking ovens still survive in Alberta's Crowsnest Pass.

with stall numbers "2" and "3" above the entrances. However, track no longer lead to the doorways. Like roundhouses, early engine houses have largely disappeared from railway landscapes, and so this is a quite unique relic. Although a rare heritage feature, the engine house remains on railway property and is not a publicly accessible attraction.

Grain Elevators, Creston, B.C.

A grain elevator is a rare find in mountainous British Columbia. While common (at one time) across the Prairie Provinces, there were few of these structures built in B.C. In all, British Columbia may have counted fewer than thirty elevators, most in the north. The concentration of these elevators in the north was due to the fact that there was little grain produced in the southern interior of that province. In fact, the two trackside grain

While once common on Canada's Prairies, grain elevators were rare in mountainous British Columbia. These survivors in Creston are the subject of preservation discussions.

elevators in Creston may be the last. Built by the Alberta Wheat Pool and United Grain Growers in 1935, they are now out of service and face demolition. The grain-growing region of northern British Columbia — an extension of the Prairies — had a few more elevators, at such places as Pouce Coupe, Dawson Creek, and Fort

St. John. Few of these function as grain elevators any longer. For instance, the former Alberta Pool elevator in Dawson Creek is now an art gallery and museum.

Laurel Packing House / BNA Tobacco Building, Kelowna, B.C.

Built in 1917, the Laurel Packing House is the last of the railway warehouses in what was Kelowna's warehouse district. At the time it was built, it was British Columbia's largest packing house. The building continued to function as a warehouse for decades, surviving a fire in the 1960s, which wiped out most of the town's old warehouse district. It retained that role until 1970, when it was slated for demolition. Happily, the town rallied to save it and designated it as a heritage building, the first such structure so designated by the town. It is now one of the oldest such heritage buildings in British Columbia. Renovated in 2010, it now houses the B.C. Orchard Industry Museum, and the B.C. Wine Museum. It stands near Ellis and Cawston streets. in Kelowna's new cultural district.

Located just a block or so away, the historic BNA Tobacco building, built in 1900, has recently opened as a brew pub. The two are within a short distance of the former Kelowna train station (also a pub). Both are solid and simple two-storey brick structures, reflecting the utilitarian nature of historic industrial buildings.

Rocky Mountaineer Station, Vancouver, B.C.

Although the spectacular *Rocky Mountaineer* tour train is a relatively new experience, its Vancouver station is housed in a heritage railway building, one built by the CNR for locomotive maintenance. The train operators have renovated the space to provide more spacious and brighter accommodation for those waiting to board the world-famous tour train. Full-length glass windows fill the former engine doors, while the cavernous interior allows travellers to take in the vastness of the former facility. The station stands on Cottrell Street near Terminal Avenue in Vancouver, only blocks from the historic Pacific Central station.

Yaletown Warehouses, Vancouver, B.C.

After the CPR relocated its yards and other facilities to the north side of False Creek a community known as Yaletown sprang up, consisting of the roundhouse, shops, and yards. The area was populated by railway workers who had relocated from Yale. Around the yards a warehouse district developed, zoned as light industrial by the city. These distinctive streets are lined with buildings that have raised platforms, built to make the loading of the freight cars easier, and canopies, created to protect the workers from the incessant winter rains. Although the workers have long gone, and the tracks no longer remain, and while today's occupants are more likely to be offices, condos, shops, and restaurants, the railway warehouses remain. There the raised freight platforms and protective canopies have been preserved, especially along Mainland and Hamilton streets, giving Yaletown its unique early railway-era landscape.

HOUSING: HOW THE RAILWAYMEN LIVED

Prior to the rise of the auto age, when other modes of transportation were far less available, railway employees needed a place to live, or to at least rest, between shifts. In many northern Ontario railway towns, the railway companies built housing for staff. The best examples are in Schreiber, Chapleau, Nakina, and Cartier. This was not normally the case in the Canadian mountains. Divisional towns did include some housing for senior staff, but train crews often ended up in noisy and drafty bunkhouses. In a few locations, the YMCA provided facilities, but these were gone by the late 1950s.

Station agents could count on having living space upstairs in their stations. This could range from two bedrooms with a living room and a kitchen in a full second floor, such as those in the Canadian Northern's third-class stations, to a simple apartment tucked into an upstairs dormer, such as those in the Grand Trunk Pacific stations. Many of the station museums have displays of such living quarters.

As the need for divisional towns dwindled with the arrival of diesel locomotives, bunkhouses were removed, or replaced with more modern buildings with up-to-date conveniences. Senior staff would often live in homes that were far more substantial.

Cranbrook, B.C.

At first glance, Cranbrook resembles a typical highway town, with a string of motels and fast food outlets along Highway 3/95. But a visit to its railway heritage area, which includes stations, a water tower, and train displays, makes its rail roots clearly apparent. The housing for the trains crews, however, is less so. The most significant heritage structure away from the museum area is the former CPR superintendent's home. Built in 1900, this home displays rooftop gables and a large veranda. It was designated as a heritage structure by the municipality in 1990 and in 2006 won the town's Commercial Heritage Award. Located on Garden Avenue, it is now a bed and breakfast. Its owners upgraded the building in 2006, and its rooms now contain suites and private baths.

A second heritage home is the Colonel Baker home, built in 1887. Although it predates the arrival of the railway, it does have a connection to the railway as the Honourable Colonel James Baker, for whom the house was built, was instrumental in the founding of Cranbrook and bringing the CPR to town. A designated heritage building, and the oldest structure in Cranbrook, the house contains a small interpretation room, although not open to the public. It is located on St. Louis Street beside Baker Park.

Field, B.C.

Although much quieter now, Field does retain a variety of heritage railway structures that date back to a time when the town was an important railway stopping place. While the CP bunkhouse has been updated in recent years, examples of staff houses remain. Among the most interesting are a pair of CPR log houses built in 1928. These storey-and-a-half buildings

survive amidst the many renovated houses which yet line the town's streets. They are situated on Burgess Street, near 2nd Avenue. Along the backstreets, several now-renovated examples of former railwaymen's houses also still stand.

Nelson, B.C.

After the CPR reached the shores of Kootenay Lake, building on what had originally been a portage railway from Arrow Lake, the steamer port of Nelson boomed. In 1902, when the CPR finally linked Nelson with its southern main line from Cranbrook via steamers on the Kootenay Lake between Proctor and Kootenay Landing, Nelson became a key railway headquarters, with a large station and office, a roundhouse, and extensive yards. The best surviving example of the town's railway residential heritage is the superintendent's house. This two-storey wooden structure, with its wrap-around porch, rests on a hill overlooking the station and railway yards. Designed by a local architect, Alexander Carrie, the house was completed in 1908 and today is listed on the town's heritage register. The town is also noted for its restored heritage main street.

North Bend, B.C.

Because it has been off the beaten path for much of its existence, the CPR divisional town of North Bend retains much of its heritage ambience. Although both the station and bunkhouse are recent structures, a pair of early high-line houses still stand.

The CPR superintendent's house in Nelson, British Columbia, is a designated heritage property.

In 1913, the CPR enhanced their management living facilities in the Fraser Valley divisional town of North Bend by building a string of eight substantial houses on a rise of land overlooking the town. Typically, the structures were built according to the CPR pattern book — two with a projecting gable above a porch; two with a bay window in the lower storey; four with an asymmetrical gable, of the kind on the last two surviving homes.

In October of 2015, a heritage-conscious Vancouver entrepreneur bought the houses from the Fraser Valley Regional District for one dollar each, on the stipulation that the exteriors be preserved. While that was agreed to, it was decided that, given their interior condition, much restoration will be required inside. Two unique examples of surviving CPR housing will thus remain a visible part of the Fraser Valley's scarce railway heritage.

The CPR management housing in North Bend is a rare example of early divisional housing.

Another piece of the town's heritage from its railway days has recently disappeared, however. A new bridge across the Fraser River has replaced the unusual aerial cable ferry which formerly was the town's only access to the highway system.

Section Houses

These simple homes, built at frequent intervals to house the railway section foremen and their families,

really did not outlast the vast changes to rail operations that began in the 1950s. Indeed, few have survived. The section house in Brookmere, which now sports the station name board, is one example. In Vernon, the CPR section house, built in 1911, stands on 30th Street, north of 39th Avenue and near the tracks close to its original location. Still retaining its Tuscan-red wood siding, it is a two-storey cross gabled home, a pre-fab from BC Mills. It is listed on Vernon's heritage property inventory.

Craigdarroch Castle was built in 1889 by coal baron and railway builder Robert Dunsmuir and reflects how the railway builders lived. It is now a National Historic Site.

A rare surviving former bunkhouse still stands in Golden B.C. across the road from the station that VIA Rail erected when the Golden CPR station was moved offsite to become a museum. Two-stories in height, it is now the Dreamcatcher Hostel. A variety of commercial structures on Golden's heritage main street date from the days when this was a significant railway hub.

Craigdarroch Castle, Victoria, B.C.

Not, of course, an example of railway housing, Craigdarroch Castle does, however, have an important connection with the railway. This stunning stone castle was the dream home of coal baron and E&N Railway builder Robert Dunsmuir. Sadly, just before its 1889 completion, Dunsmuir passed away, and so he never lived to see his dream.

The thirty-nine-room castle incorporated more than twenty-thousand square feet of floor space.

Construction material included brick, a sandstone facade, granite, and terra cotta tile from San Francisco. The interior featured an oak staircase which was prefabricated in Chicago, stained-glass windows, Italian marble, and Vermont slate. Designed by Warren Williams, it is described as a "bonanza castle" — a building intentionally intended to flaunt the owner's wealth, and indeed Dunsmuir was British Columbia's wealthiest man at the time. Following the death of his widow, Joan, in 1908, the contents were auctioned off and the acreage subdivided into housing lots. The mansion served as a military hospital following the First World War, and later as a music conservancy. It was designated as a National Historic Site in 1992, and is now a museum. It sits atop a hill on Joan Crescent in Victoria.

Hatley Castle, Victoria, B.C.

In a case of like father like son, the Dunsmuirs created yet another palatial home in Victoria. In 1908, Robert's son, James, commissioned Victoria architect Sam McClure to create a turreted castle on what is today the grounds of Royal Roads University. Echoing his father, James declared, "Money doesn't matter, just build what I want." And that is exactly what McClure did. Two hundred feet long and eighty-six feet wide, with an eighty-two-foot turret, Hatley Park, as he called it, was one of Victoria's grandest homes. But James didn't stop there. He also hired Boston landscape architects Brett and Hall to create an extensive garden on the grounds around the building. The grounds also contained stables, silos, a slaughter house, and accommodation for his extensive staff of stable hands and servants.

In 1910, James sold the E&N railway to the Canadian Pacific Railway, and retired to his estate. James Dunsmuir died in 1920, while his wife, Laura, and daughter, Eleanor, lived on in the empty building until Laura died in 1937. The Canadian government then bought the building for a naval training facility. In 1968 it became known as the Royal Roads Military College. In 1994, when the college closed, the B.C. government purchased the property and opened Royal Roads University. Today, both the estate museum and gardens are available for special events and for guided walking tours. The entrance to the grounds is from Highway 14A, three kilometres from exit 10 on the Trans-Canada Highway.

SHIPS

S.S. *Moyie* and S.S. *Kaslo*

From the heritage city of Nelson, with its revitalized main street and large historic wooden station, steamships connected the CPR docks with Kaslo and the mine in Sandon. Until 1958, the sternwheeler S.S. *Moyie* puffed between Kaslo and the docks at Nelson. Prefabricated in Toronto, the *Moyie* was intended to service the Stikine River and Teslin Lake in the Klondike, but ended up on Kootenay Lake in 1898 instead. The world's oldest intact passenger sternwheeler, it has since been declared a National Historic Site and has become a museum in Kaslo. A half-size replica also operates in Calgary's Heritage Park.

S.S. *Sicamous*

Situated in Penticton's Heritage Park is the S.S. *Sicamous*. Like the *Moyie*, it shuttled produce and people, sailing between CPR railway docks along the Okanagan Lake. Built by the CPR and launched in 1914 with the arrival of the KVR, it operated until 1951. Its lavish interior included a twenty-metre-long dining room, skylights, staterooms, and brass fittings. It operated as a museum from 1951 to 1965, and then housed a restaurant until 1987, when restorations began. It became a National Historic Site in 1989. Today, it has been restored by the S.S. *Sicamous* Restoration Society, the Gyro Club, and the Penticton Museum. It is a popular museum, reflecting the roles played by steamer and rail service in the Okanagan area. It is located in the S.S. *Sicamous* Heritage Park on Riverside Drive on the much-renovated Lake Okanagan waterfront.

Canada is fortunate that so many museums and heritage organizations cherish this country's railway heritage. Museums dedicated to this legacy flourish from coast to coast, in every province and territory (except for the Northwest Territories and Nunavut, which had no railways). Because the mountains of western Canada contain such a colourful railway heritage, it comes as no surprise that many of our country's most extensive railway museums and collections are to be found here.

Canadian Museum of Rail Travel, Cranbrook, B.C.

The museum is named the "Trains Deluxe" for a reason. The highly regarded Canadian Museum of Rail Travel in the heart of Cranbrook displays some of the most luxurious train sets that the CPR ever operated, depicting what were the true glory years of rail travel in western Canada. For example, on Track 1 is the ultra-luxurious *Trans Canada Limited* train set, with its four sleeper cars, parlour car, diner, and lounge car — cars that were given glamorous names such as the Argyle, the Somerset, the River Rouge, and the Rutherglen. It represents the complete and only surviving set of this, the epitome of the glamorous days of rail travel. It operated between 1919 and 1930 over the CPR's main line from Montreal to Vancouver.

The four-coach train set, the *Soo-Spokane Train Deluxe*, rests on the adjacent track. This train operated between 1907 and 1914 and included Cranbrook on its route from Portland to Minneapolis.

Track 3 contains the only four surviving cars from the 1936 lightweight *Chinook* train set. Here too sit a collection of business cars, royal cars, and cars of state.

Part of the new display building houses one of the more unusual feats of railway preservation, and that is the relocation and preservation of the luxurious Royal Alexandra Hall, built in 1906 for the now-demolished CPR Royal Alexandra Hotel in Winnipeg. It was known as the "Café" or the "European Dining Room." Disassembled and moved

Several heritage trains sets are open for public viewing at the Canadian Museum of Rail Travel in Cranbrook, British Columbia.

When the CPR's Royal Alexandra Hotel was demolished in Winnipeg, its historic café was rescued and reassembled at the Canadian Museum of Rail Travel in Cranbrook, British Columbia.

piece-by-piece from its storage, it was reassembled in Cranbrook and now serves as an event venue.

The City of Cranbrook has recognized its deep rail roots by designating a "Railway Heritage Area," which also contains a 1948 wooden water tower, a CPR locomotive display, and the relocated Elko CPR station, the only surviving example of the Crowsnest Pass station pattern. Across the railyards, but not accessible to the public, is the surviving portion of the CPR roundhouse.

Other than the reconstructed Royal Alexandra Hall, the main museum is a new structure, although adjacent is the original CPR freight shed. The reconstructed, but now vacant, CPR station lies nearby.

The Trains Deluxe website (www.trainsdeluxe.com) offers excellent interactive maps and information about the trains and the area's heritage as well.

BC Forest Discovery Centre, Duncan, B.C.

This extensive display of British Columbia's forestry and railway heritage began as a passion of Gerry Wellburn in Duncan on Vancouver Island. Since then, the museum collection has ballooned to include five thousand forestry-related artifacts, plus locomotives and heritage buildings. Today, the centre covers more than forty hectares and includes an operating railway and nature trails. Its mission is to collect and preserve artifacts relating to the history of B.C. coastal forestry, and these include the vital narrow-gauge logging trains.

Most of the rolling stock originates from logging or forest operations, much of which pre-dates the Second World War. Its collection of 36-inch gauge locomotives include a pair of 0-4-0 Vulcan steam locomotives dating from 1906 and 1910. Number 25 is known as the *Samson*. The Bloedel Stewart and Welch Shay locomotive was built in 1911; the Hillcrest locomotive dates from 1920;

the Shawinigan Lake Lumber Company from 1910; Hillcrest Lumber Company, 1915; and three Plymouth locomotives date from the 1920s. Visitors can climb onto one of three open coaches for a ride behind one of the steam engines or a speeder or gas locomotive when the steam engine is not working.

Train rides, which include passage across the Somenos Lake Trestle, operate from early April until the end of September, although the Samson steam locomotive operates weekends only during the summer. Special excursions occur throughout the year. Heritage buildings are logging related and include a 1930s logging camp along with bunkhouse, dining hall, post office, and blacksmith shop. The museum is on Highway #1 in Duncan, north of Victoria.

Prince George Railway and Forestry Museum

Among the largest in British Columbia, the Prince George Railway and Forestry Museum began modestly in 1983 with the restoration of a 1903 Russell snowplough from the Northwood Pulp and Timber Limited, which is how a railway museum ended up with "Forestry" in its name. By the time it opened in 1986, to coincide with Vancouver's TransExpo 86, the collection had grown to forty rail cars and locomotives.

Located behind the current CN locomotive shops, the museum grounds now offer a wide variety of historic railway items. Among them is steam locomotive #1520, built in 1906 for the Canadian Northern Railway and on display at Montreal's Canadian Railway Museum until 1991, when the PGRF museum acquired it. In addition, seven vintage diesel locomotives are on display, including

a twenty-five-ton locomotive, and a blue, white, and red BC Rail electric locomotive rescued from the CN storage yard. Visitors will also see a 1948 Louisiana Pacific yard switcher. Fourteen passenger coaches include sleepers, some of which date back to 1913 and many of which are from the 1920s, and more than forty freight cars, the oldest of which was built for the GTR in 1912. Box cars, cabooses, flat cars, snowploughs, and tank cars round out the collection. Forestry-related displays include a sawmill beehive waste burner and a fire tower.

Among the historic buildings on site are the GTP rural-pattern station, originally from Penny, B.C., and the smaller Pacific Great Eastern station from Hixon, B.C. The grounds also include restored CN bunkhouses, a relocated turntable from the CN's Prince George yard, a small section house, and the main building, which was built to resemble the historic GTP station at McBride. A miniature railway called the Cottonwood Railway hauls children (and kids at heart) around the landscaped grounds.

The museum is located on River Road just north of the large CN yards.

Revelstoke Railway Museum

As Revelstoke was a key link in the CPR's western main line, it is only fitting that it should boast one of the West's major railway museums. With its dozen or so pieces of rolling stock, it is notably smaller than the museums in Prince George or Squamish, but it has the advantage of being adjacent to one of the CPR's busiest and most historic railway locations. In addition to a variety of freight and maintenance equipment, it also shows off its 1948 2-8-2 CPR Mikado steam locomotive, built in 1948 as the steam era was nearing its end. Displays in the museum depict the harsh conditions that faced the railway builders in the treacherous mountain passes. The museum itself was built to look like a rail-yard back shop. It is located on the appropriately named Track Street a few blocks from Revelstoke's historic downtown.

West Coast Railway Heritage Park, Squamish, B.C.

In 1961, a small but determined band of eleven rail enthusiasts set out to preserve the province's neglected railway heritage and succeeded in building a collection of ninety pieces of rolling stock, the oldest being an 1890 CPR business car. The collection includes a number of train sets, including a five-coach CN passenger train, a seven-coach CPR train, and a three-car Pacific Great Eastern train including a troop coach, as well as a freight train. Among the steam locomotives are a 1910 PGE 2-6-2 steam locomotive and, the jewel in the crown, the famous 2860 *Royal Hudson* steam locomotive. (Alas it is not the one which carried King George VI and Queen Elizabeth on their cross-country pre-war tour in 1939. That was # 2850. The "royal" name came from King George, who so liked the engine's performance that he gave permission to the CPR to name no fewer than sixty-three locomotives of that style "royal.")

Oddities include the "Grey Ghost," a 1937 Ford automobile on train wheels used as an inspection car, and the Sweet Apple "station," built for the 1995 TV

One of the few surviving Royal Hudson *steam locomotives is part of the collection in the West Coast Railway Heritage Park in Squamish, British Columbia.*

movie *Bye Bye Birdie*, but which remains in place. In a way, the Squamish "station" is odd as well. Although it was designed in 1915 to be the PGE's Squamish station, it was not built until the museum adopted the plans to construct the structure as the centrepiece for the museum.

One of Canada's most extensive collections of railway equipment lies at the West Coast Railway Heritage Park in Squamish, British Columbia.

Every rail yard needs a turntable and roundhouse. Here the roundhouse was built not just to house the collection, but also includes a conference centre and the usual gift shop.

Historic Engine #374, Vancouver, B.C.

While this museum consists of a single piece of rolling stock, that single piece represents arguably the most significant chapter in the history of western Canada's railway. Number 374 is the CPR locomotive that hauled the first passenger train from across the country into the new railway town of Vancouver in 1887, thus ensuring Canada's status as a nation.

Along with seven other similar locomotives, #374, with its 4-4-0 wheel configuration and sixty-nine-inch driving wheels, rolled out of the CPR's Montreal

CPR #374 was the first engine to pull into the CPR's West Coast terminal of Vancouver.

shops in 1886 and, along with #371, was sent west to operate between North Bend and the then terminus of Port Moody. Engine 371 actually hauled the first trans-continental train, pulling it into Port Moody in July of 1886. Then, the following year, #374 made its historic journey, bringing the first cross country passenger train into the new terminal at Vancouver.

While #371 was scrapped in 1915, #374 was rebuilt and operated until 1945 when the CPR donated it to the Vancouver Park Board. Sadly, the city left it to languish at Kitsilano Beach for thirty-eight years, subject to weathering and vandalism. In 1981, the West Coast Railway Association and the Canadian Railroad Historical Association moved it into a warehouse on Granville Island, where members spent two years restoring its appearance. It was put on display at Expo 86 at the historic CPR Drake Street roundhouse in Vancouver. But even then its future looked uncertain. Happily, when

Concord Pacific bought the Expo lands for new development, they retained the roundhouse, converting it to a community centre and donating it to the city. The Vancouver Board of Parks and Recreation erected a new glass pavilion adjacent to the roundhouse and #374 now has a glass-encased showroom all to itself.

TRAIN DISPLAYS

These grand and informative museums are not the only examples of heritage railway displays. Throughout the western mountains, one finds many locomotives, coaches, and other displays of heritage railway equipment.

Bankhead, AB

Located within Banff National Park is a ghost town with a small railway display. Bankhead, situated five kilometres north of Banff, was a prosperous coal mining town that extracted the vital coal for the steam locomotives. With the demise of steam, the mines closed, and the buildings were removed, leaving only a field of foundations. Visitors can walk among them with the aid of historic plaques. Here too is a small mining train, with a 4-4-0 Porter locomotive built in 1905, and four coal cars. The Bankhead station is now a hostel in the town of Banff.

Britannia Mine, B.C.

The Britannia Mine operated from 1904 to 1974 and was the largest copper mine in the British Empire. This remarkably well-preserved mine and townsite, home

to sixty thousand workers and their families over its sixty-year lifespan, is now a National Historic Site. Its legacy and attractions involve not so much the railway but one of Canada's largest mine operations, one worthy of a separate chapter on its own. Its role in the railway heritage of the West is limited to an extensive display of ore cars, flat cars, and an explosives car, along with a 24-inch gauge Porter steam locomotive from 1908, and a variety of 24-inch gauge diesel locomotives relocated from a variety of other locations. Most are displayed inside the vast smelter building.

Part of the reason for the site's well-preserved status is that, until the PGE railway from North Vancouver to Britannia and Squamish was completed in 1958, the townsite and mine had no land access. However, today the site is now on a busy four-lane highway and has become a must-see tourist attraction. Many of the original company buildings still line the streets of the townsite.

Burnaby Village Museum, Burnaby, B.C.

One of the many historic displays available in this collection of historic structures is the restored interurban tramcar #1223. It was part of the BC Electric Railway interurban system, which operated on the Lower Mainland from 1913 to 1958. The tramcar was one of roughly one thousand such vehicles turned out by the St. Louis Car Company, thirty-two of which were purchased by the BCER.

The Burnaby Historical Society managed to save it from the scrapyard, one of only seven not scrapped, displaying it at Edmunds Loop in Burnaby; however, vandals unfortunately damaged it. It was finally moved to the safety of the Burnaby Village Museum. Although this location was safer, the car still remained subject to the damp elements of the coast. In 2000, the Friends of Interurban #1223 got to work on a major restoration. It is now safely protected from the elements in its new car barn. Standing beside the new car barn is a typical BCER interurban station, which formerly stood at Vorce.

Located on Deer Lake Avenue, the heritage village has been around since 1971 and includes nearly forty heritage buildings and other facilities, including a restored 1912 C.W. Parker Carousel.

Fort Steele Railway Company, Fort Steele, AB

Besides the many heritage buildings in the "ghost town" of Fort Steele, a provincially designated heritage site, the town offers a display of railway equipment. Visitors can view all of this and even take a ride on its steam locomotive, the 1923 #1077, a 2-6-2 engine once belonging to Victoria Lumbering and Manufacturing Company. Engine #1 dates from 1910 and operated for the Elk River Colliery and other coal companies in Fernie. A 1922 Plymouth and a 1930 three-truck Shay round out the exhibit, along with various flat cars and coal cars. During the summer, the steam train pulls tourists along a scenic route near the town.

Sullivan Mine Interpretive Centre, Kimberley, B.C.

Part of the rail tour on the Kimberley Underground Mining Railway is the Sullivan Mine Interpretive Centre, part of which was one of Canada's largest underground

mines, with 500 kilometres of underground tunnels including 1700 metres of rail. It all dates to 1909, when the CPR mine, operating as the Consolidated Mining and Smelting Company, began producing lead, zinc, and silver. The mine produced ore of a value of over $20 billion before it closed in 2001. Over that time, it was British Columbia's most valuable mine. Exhibits cover more than sixty hectares and include a school house, a miner's residence, and the mine's large powerhouse, where information is provided on the mine operation and history. Railway displays include four 18-inch gauge 1908 mine mules, and three others from 1914, all of which operated in the mine. Other mining railway equipment includes ore cars, flat cars, an explosives car, and an ambulance car (something that goes with the explosives car, naturally), most of which display the typical 36-inch gauge of mining rail equipment.

Kaatza Station Museum and Archives, Lake Cowichan, B.C.

Using the decommissioned E&N (CPR) Lake Cowichan station, the Kaatza Historical Society has assembled an extensive archive of material from the logging, mining, and farming days in the Lake Cowichan area. Included is a display of rail equipment, consisting of a 1927 Shay locomotive, a 1927 Plymouth locomotive, as well as a logging car and 1916 caboose, all of which line up on a track beside the 1913 wooden station. The archives contain five thousand photos and a great deal of written information on the many local logging companies. The station and display lie on South Shore Road in the town of Lake Cowichan, less than 30 kilometres from Duncan and 110 from Victoria.

Ladysmith, B.C.

Formerly located beside the Ladysmith Railway Museum, a small display of rail equipment now resides near the Ladysmith Waterfront Arts Centre. These include a 2-8-2 1923 steam locomotive with the name "Comox Logging Railway" on its side, a passenger car, logging cars, and a wooden boxcar. The 1941 CPR station itself is boarded up, however — the victim of local vandals.

Lake Louise, AB

After the lovely log station at Lake Louise was protected under the HRSPA in 1990, it became a fine-dining restaurant. To enhance the railway theme, the owners bought a trio of passenger cars from the Tuscan Club in Toronto in 1993. These included the diner coach, the *Killarney*, built in 1906 as a CP official car (an abbreviated form of its business cars that CP built for special use by its officials); a 1921 dining car, the *Laurentian*, which awaits restoration; and the 1921 *Delamere*, another former CP official car, which has now been fitted up for dining and special occasions.

National Railway Historical Association, B.C. Chapter, New Westminster, B.C.

The hard-working B.C. chapter of the National Railway Historical Association has, since 1935, assembled an impressive collection of railway equipment, primarily CN, CP, and VIA coaches and baggage cars, some of which date back to the 1920s. Many of these have been carefully restored. As of 2015, the chapter is working with local municipalities to acquire property on which to display this remarkable collection. The collection is currently stored in a New Westminster warehouse, but it is available for weddings and various events.

Alberni Pacific Railway, Port Alberni, B.C.

In 1980, the Western Vancouver Island Industrial Heritage Society decided enough was enough and organized to help save some of the island's vanishing railway heritage. First up was a 1912 Shay logging locomotive known as the "2-spot." The society then turned its attention to a steam donkey from the Port Alberni mill and then a large steam locomotive, the 1929 Baldwin 2-8-2, which is now used to haul the society's tour trains. Although the operating coaches are really converted CN cabooses, the society also has an 1882 Credit Valley Railway parlour car.

Sandon, B.C.

British Columbia's ghost towns seem to have a habit of attracting railway displays. This is certainly the case in one of the province's more genuine ghost towns, the one-time silver mining town of Sandon. Located deep in the mountains north of Nelson, two rail lines made their way up the narrow valley to the booming townsite — the CPR and Kaslo and Slocan Railways — both of which located stations there. But following the closing of the mines and a devastating flood, the town was left deserted, with little left behind but vacant structures. However, these soon began to attract curious visitors. A historical society was established and a tourist office opened. Beginning in 1995, railway equipment began to arrive, and the collection there today consists of a 1908 CPR steam locomotive, behind which are two box cars, two flat cars, and a tank car. These pieces do not display spit and polish — in fact, a sign on the locomotive indicates that restoration is still under way — but they do help vividly recall the railway and the mining history of this intriguing ghost town.

Across the street sits a fleet of decommissioned buses: another legacy of the area's past transportation legacy.

Sandon Road leads from Highway 31A north of Nelson to the ghost town. Once in the town, Idaho Peak Road leads to the upper townsite and the railway display, along with the K&S station.

Three Valley Gap, West of Revelstoke, B.C.

This tourist attraction, located on the Trans-Canada Highway a short distance west of Revelstoke, bills itself as a "Heritage Ghost Town and Transportation Museum." It is not however a "ghost town," since Three Valley Gap is not a once-existing real town that has now been abandoned. Rather, it is an assembly of heritage buildings that have been relocated here from other places, places that themselves may have been vacated. Among the twenty-five heritage structures are shops and businesses of the type that were once typically found in small-town Canada, such as a blacksmith, a watchmaker, and so on.

Strangely, despite its location adjacent to the CPR main line, there is no railway station. There is, however, a modern, twenty-four-bay "roundhouse," built specifically to house a variety of historic railway equipment. Sitting around the turntable are a 2-6-2 logging locomotive dating from 1912, as well as a 30-inch gauge 0-4-0 industrial locomotive dating from 1922. Various other pieces of equipment include coaches, sleepers, business

and official cars dating from the 1920s to the 1950s, although not all are on display at the same time.

Adjacent to the site is the Three Valley Lake Chateau, a newly opened chateau-style hotel, which overlooks the waters of Three Valley Lake. Auto lovers will enjoy vintage Model Ts and other historic vehicles in the Three Valley Gap Antique Automobile Museum.

Other railway displays around Canada's western mountains include a 1920 mining locomotive at the Suma-Matsqui-Abbotsford Museum in Clayburn. Prolific railway author, Adolf Hungry Wolf put his love of railways to work and assembled a small collection of three cabooses and five vintage boxcars in his Rocky Mountain Freight Train Museum at Skookumchuk. This collection is held by a private family foundation and, unfortunately is not open to the public.

A typical station agent's office has been created in the historic CPR station in Midway, British Columbia.

THE RAIL TRAILS

f there is an upside to the end of the rail era, and the abandonment of the rail lines, it is that today's generation can follow the network of rail trails that follow the old road beds, and get some vigorous exercise while doing it. Here cyclists and hikers can put themselves into the cab of the locomotives, as it were, and witness the scenery that train engineers themselves would have experienced without having to worry about the snowdrifts, the avalanches, and the derailments that the trainmen confronted. Many of the trails follow scenic rivers and lakeshores, plunge into dark tunnels, and pass high above deep and dizzying canyons. Most of the rail trails form part of the vast Trans Canada Trail network. Indeed, some of North America's most prized and spectacular rail trails are those that await them in the mountains and the valleys of the Canadian West.

NORTH STAR TRAIL, KIMBERLEY TO CRANBROOK, 26 KM

This line that linked North Star, on the CPR's southern main line, to the Sullivan Mine in Kimberley was opened in 1899 under the charter of the British Columbia Southern Railway, a CPR line, and was known as the North Star branch. It was built to provide access to the smelters at Marysville as well as the Sullivan Mine in Kimberley. The line was eventually closed in 2009. Today, the paved trail, popular with families and commuters, stretches twenty-six kilometres from the Kimberley Civic Centre to North Star junction on the CPR just outside of Cranbrook.

Heading south from Kimberley, the trail encounters the Wycliffe Prairie, an open area that takes in views of the Rocky Mountains to the east. The trail gradually descends for eighteen kilometres before it comes to the steel-girder bridge over the St. Mary River. The Cranbrook trailhead lies on McPhee Road and Theatre Road at the north end of Cranbrook.

SLOCAN VALLEY RAIL TAIL, NELSON TO SLOCAN, 45 KM

This scenic forty-five-kilometre rail trail traces the route of the CPR's Columbia and Kootenay Railway from its junction with the CPR's southern main line west of Nelson, a point known as South Slocan, to the once busy mining town and steamer port of Slocan, following the scenic valley of the Slocan River.

The C&KR began operations in 1897. The CPR chartered the line as a way of competing with the intrusive American-owned rail lines such as the Nelson and Fort Sheppard Railway, built by Daniel Corbin to Nelson in 1893. Ore trains would haul the mined ore from Nelson to the steamer terminal at Slocan, where barges would then carry the bounty to Rosebery and then by rail to the smelters at Revelstoke. But with the closing of the Revelstoke smelters, the line became redundant — it was nicknamed the "railway from nowhere to nowhere" — and the CPR abandoned it in 1993, donating the right of way to the Trans Canada Trail Foundation.

The southern trailhead lies beside Highway 3A, west of Nelson at the Dam Inn Pub. A short distance along, the trail encounters perhaps the only building that can trace its age to the coming of the railway, the Frog Peak Café, which is situated in a building erected in 1896. The first few kilometres of the trail are decidedly urban, until the trail reaches the Slocan Valley, where it follows the roadbed northwesterly. Here lies a more rural and wooded area, and the trail climbs the hillside and offers views of the valley. It follows the Crescent Valley to Passmore, sixteen kilometres farther on. Between Passmore and Winlaw, roughly ten kilometres, the trail hugs the river, providing a more bucolic route for cyclists and hikers, free of development.

Winlaw, a former railway town, offers trail users cafes and shopping. "Winlaw Station" is a modern storage facility for trail maintenance. At Lemon Creek, the trail encounters more urban amenities then passes through open farm land. About one kilometre before entering Lemon Creek, an open field marks the site of one of British Columbia's Second World War Japanese internment camps. A plaque marks the site of the remains of many such camps — camps that were created during the sad era when Canadians of Japanese ancestry were considered "enemy aliens" and placed in remote locations while their property was confiscated.

Nearing Slocan, the trail will cross a rail trestle decked in for trail use. It then passes the site of another internment camp before going through a wildlife sanctuary and ending in Slocan, a one-time ferry and barge terminal on the south end of Slocan Lake. Until 1993, CPR freight cars were shunted onto barges for the trip to Rosebery and the short hop to Nakusp, where barges again waited for the journey to the landing at Arrowhead and on into Revelstoke. Now largely a residential community, Slocan has retained scant evidence of that railway heritage.

Facilities on the route include the Lemon Creek Lodge, and, at Winlaw, the aptly named "Sleep is for Sissies" — it was a place famous for its parties. Several access points lie along the forty-five-kilometre route. Highway 3A largely parallels the old rail line.

The Salmo, British Columbia, train station is a feature along the Great Northern Rail Trail in southern British Columbia.

GREAT NORTHERN RAIL TRAIL, NELSON TO SALMO, 40.6 KM

In 1893, the American rail building icon, Daniel Chase Corbin, managed to extend his Great Northern Railway from Spokane, Washington across the border and on to Nelson on Kootenay Lake, much to the chagrin of the CPR, which was then working on its southern main line at the time to prevent just such an incursion. The Great Northern Railway followed the valley of Beaver Creek to the shore of the lake. However, the CPR's charter of the Columbia and Kootenay forced Corbin to end his tracks at Troup Junction, eight kilometres short of Nelson itself. In 1941, passenger service ended and the line was abandoned. All rail traffic ceased in 1989 and ten years later the rails were removed.

Today, the portion between Salmo and Troup Junction now forms the Great Northern Rail Trail. The trail stretches for 40.6 kilometres. The route follows the creek valley. The southern trailhead lies at the historic GN Salmo station; the northern trailhead is at Mountain Station Road in Nelson where a large parking lot and information kiosk announces the start of the trail. Along the route, the trail passes through the wooded highlands south of Nelson before arriving at the community of Porto Rico. It descends to follow the valley of Beaver Creek where it passes the rustic village of Ymir, which, with its old hotel and heritage fire hall, is but a ghost of what it was during its glory-filled mining days. The southern half of the route from Hall Siding to Salmo is shared with all-terrain vehicles and is considered more rugged and difficult for cyclists than the northern half. In addition, the southern portion is often closed during the spring due to the likelihood of encountering foraging grizzly bears.

COLUMBIA AND WESTERN / TRANS CANADA TRAIL, CASTLEGAR TO MIDWAY, 162 KM

In 1890, the CPR chartered a railway company known as the Columbia and Kootenay to build that portion of the CPR's southern main line from Castlegar to Midway, from which point the Kettle Valley Railway extended the CPR's southern main line to Hope. That section of track was abandoned in 1978, while the section from Midway to Castlegar was removed in 1990.

Now another of southern B.C.'s scenic rail trails, this 162-kilometre former mining line runs from the Castlegar Station museum to the old Fife station on the shore of Christina Lake. From the Castlegar Museum the trail follows Arrow Lake Road, beside which tracks remain in place, to its end just beyond the International Paper Products plant, where the existing tracks end. From there, the trail carries on along the railway roadbed itself, westerly to the station site of Coykendal. Here the trail begins to follow the shore of Lower Arrow Lake, where views from the ascending roadbed extend up and down the scenic forested valley. The trail bends sharply south across the Monashee Mountains reaching the shores of Christina Lake at Fife, where a former station shelter stands. From here, the trail becomes part of the Trans Canada Trail, heading westward, passing the site of Cascade City, now a ghost town.

After crossing the planked-in, two-span truss bridge over the river, the trail then meets the historic Grand Forks station, now a pub and restaurant. At the 108-kilometre mark, the trail passes the former divisional point of Eholt, which once had an eight-stall engine house, coal dock, and water tower, as well as a divisional station. No evidence of the railway and very little of the town remains today.

Although Greenwood, the next town on the line, began as a mining boom town, the railway did pass through the place. Greenwood yet reflects that boom-town legacy with a string of early stores, including the elegant former hotel.

From there, the trail follows the old rail line to Midway and the old line's junction with Mile 0 of the Kettle Valley Rail Trail. Midway features a preserved heritage station and museum, which includes an old caboose.

For the most part the trail is rough gravel, suitable primarily for mountain bikes, but it is also used by all-terrain vehicles. A few tunnels and bridges appear along the route, including a rare stone-arch tunnel at Porcupine Creek as well as a high steel truss bridge over Farr Creek.

The CPR station in Midway, British Columbia — a common CPR pattern — marks Mile 0 for the Kettle Valley Rail Trail.

KETTLE VALLEY RAIL TRAIL, MIDWAY TO HOPE, 600 KM

Following the legendary route of the Kettle Valley Railway, the KVR Rail Trail is known throughout the cycling world as one the longest and most spectacular. The six-hundred-kilometre route runs between Hope and Midway.

With the mountain ranges angling north-south, and the KVR needing to travel east west, the route had to follow a circuitous route around such mountain ranges as the Purcell Range of the Columbia Mountains and the Cascade Range of the Coast Mountains.

Despite the usual gentle grade which the railways required, usually around 2.2 percent, the trail is not uniformly easy. Grooming ranges from paved to course gravel. ATVs and even logging trucks can confront the cyclist or the hiker. For the most part, the trail is managed by either the B.C. government or the Trans

The Kettle Valley Rail Trail is one of North America's most renowned, encompassing varying elevations.

Canada Trail, although a few sections pass through First Nations land.

The KVR opened to traffic in 1915, thus completing CPR's southern main-line link from its railhead at Midway to main-line junctions at Hope and Merritt. In 1931, the CPR formally took over the KVR. Then, with the development of better roads for automobiles and trucks, rail traffic dwindled and finally halted altogether. From Midway to Hope, the track was lifted in 1978;

that from Castlegar to Midway was removed in 1990. Only those tracks operated by the Kettle Valley Steam Railway remain in place.

Midway was so named since it was the mid-point of a pioneer wagon trail known as the Dewdney Trail. Midway is also known as "Mile 0" of the Kettle Valley Rail Trail, and here, fittingly, stands a preserved CPR station.

From Midway, the rough KVR trail follows the Kettle River first westerly and then along its banks as the river bends to the north. After seventy-one kilometres the trail enters Beaverdell, where a historic two-storey hotel, built in 1901 and said to have been British Columbia's oldest, burned in 2011 under suspicious circumstances. The trail then continues on the winding roadbed for a farther sixty kilometres until it comes to the first of the eighteen Myra Canyon Trestles. The steep, bowl-shaped Myra Canyon rises more than one thousand metres above the Okanagan Valley, and posed one of the more challenging engineering obstacles for Andrew McCulloch, the KVR's chief engineer. At the eastern approach to the canyon, a large parking lot offers restrooms.

A short distance along the trestle trail itself, west of the parking area, an information board outlines the building and re-building of the fire-damaged historic trestles. Fear of heights may be an issue as some of the trestles loom dizzyingly high above the creeks that trickle below.

For those who manage to conquer the trestles, a few kilometres from the Myra Canyon Trestles the Chute Lake Resort offers rest and respite for weary cyclists. From there, so steep is the descent from the mountains to the waters of Okanagan Lake that two lengthy horseshoe curves were required. On the descent, trail users may encounter rare rock ovens, large stone ovens erected by the KVR railway contractors to heat their food in these remote mountain heights.

A little over forty kilometres from Chute Lake, the trail enters the streets of Penticton. Two railway relics here include the large 1940s Penticton yard station, now surrounded by suburban sprawl, and, by the lake, the preserved sternwheeler the S.S. *Sicamous*, which linked the railway to terminals around the lake.

From Penticton to the Prairie Valley Station, home of the popular Kettle Valley Steam Railway, the trail leaves the KVR behind, following local roads and highways instead. From Faulder, west of the steam railway, the trail resumes on the KVR roadbed, making its way through Bankier and then downhill into Princeton, nearly ninety kilometres from Faulder. Here the trail encounters a pair of trestles over Trout Creek. The old Princeton railway station has become a fast food restaurant.

From Princeton, the KVR Trail heads up the Tullameen River valley, passing such natural formations as hoodoos (freestanding rock spires caused by erosion) and the red cliffs of the canyon. Nineteen kilometres later, it enters the historic coal mining community of Coalmont, a remnant of its former glory, which features the restored Coalmont Hotel. Eight kilometres later, the trail reaches Tullameen on Otter Lake and then follows the shoreline to a wooden trestle over the narrow lake.

Between Tullameen and Brookmere, the trail passes through bucolic farmland where many log barns reflect the early days of settlement. About thirty kilometres from Otter Lake, the trail enters one of the more historic railway vestiges of the route, the one-time divisional town of Brookmere. It was here that the KVR's two main subdivisions split, the northerly portion which led to Merritt, and the southerly portion to Hope. In the middle of the junction stood the two-sided water tower and the station. Happily, the tower has survived. The station is, however, gone — only the station's name board remains, now affixed to the side of the former section house.

A short distance west of Brookmere, the trail encounters the Coquihalla Highway, which has taken over much of the old railway roadbed. The trail here only

The spectacular Quintette Tunnels near Hope, British Columbia, form part of the Kettle Valley Rail Trail.

intermittently traces the old roadbed, leading to the Quintette Tunnels, and passing Shakespearean station names like Juliet, Romeo, Portia, Jessica, Lear, and Iago.

In Coquihalla Canyon Provincial Park, the trail encounters the stunning Quintette Tunnels (there are only four of them), which are built into the sheer granite cliffs of the ninety-metre-high Coquihalla Canyon. The tunnels are considered to be one of the railway's more astounding engineering accomplishments — works,

which, along with the Myra Canyon Trestles, earned the KVR the name "McCulloch's Wonder."

From the tunnels, the KVR Trail then follows the Kettle Valley Road into the busy town of Hope. Here the line linked with the CPR, thus completing its southern main line.

In Hope, the KVR crossed the Canadian Northern Railway (now the CNR.) The former Hope CNR station now sits in a new location beside the highway, while traffic shares the railway bridge across the wide Fraser River.

GALLOPING GOOSE TRAIL, LEECHTOWN TO VICTORIA, 55 KM

Situated in the interior of southern Vancouver Island, the Galloping Goose Trail follows an abandoned CNR rail corridor from downtown Victoria for fifty-five kilometres to the vanished village of Leechtown.

The portion of the trail near Leechtown passes Potholes Provincial Park, noted for its "potholes" — a geological term for depressions in bedrock that are caused by hard boulders, caught in the swirling eddies of a river, grinding out holes in the softer bedrock.

At the twelve-kilometre mark, Todd Creek Trestle is a rare surviving wooden trestle, rising high above Todd Creek. Charters Trestle is a steel trestle, found at roughly the forty-six-kilometre mark. As the trail passes Matheson Lake, the scenery becomes more dramatic with rocky cliffs soaring high overhead.

But from Langford into Victoria the trail leaves behind the scenic countryside and passes through urban sprawl and the trail is occasionally hard to pick out among the many roads and pathways. As it enters the outskirts of Victoria, the trail comes to the Switch Bridge over the Trans-Canada Highway. Here the trail forms a junction with the Lochside Trail, which leads to Schwartz Bay. (This latter abandoned CNR branch is a largely urbanized twenty-nine-kilometre path). Coming closer to downtown Victoria, the trail crosses the Selkirk Trestle, a three-hundred-metre-long wooden trestle over the Selkirk Inlet and ends at the Johnson Street Bridge, site of the former station.

COWICHAN VALLEY TRAIL, DUNCAN TO LAKE COWICHAN, 60 KM

Following abandoned sections of the former CN and CP branch lines to Lake Cowichan, the trail is a sixty-kilometre loop trail. Most of the route takes in the forests of the Vancouver Island's interior and includes the Marie Canyon Trestle as well as the stunning Kinsol Trestle, said to be the largest of its kind remaining in the world.

From Sherman Road in Duncan, the trail follows the CPR roadbed to Lake Cowichan and is well surfaced. This branch line was built by the E&N (later the CPR) in 1886 and abandoned in 1982. After leaving the Duncan area, the trail enters the forests of the interior, crossing the steel trestle over Lake Cowichan River after twenty-seven kilometres. After twenty-eight kilometres, the trail reaches Lake Cowichan and the shelter that announces the Trans Canada Trail trailhead. Here, fittingly, the trail user will encounter the Kaatza CPR station museum and railway display.

From Lake Cowichan, the rail trail loops onto the former CNR right of way, which has a rougher surface than that over the CPR line. Rail service lasted here from 1922 until 1983. Within a short distance from Lake Cowichan, the trail crosses two short trestles, that over the Fairview Creek and the 70 Mile trestle. About ten kilometres from Lake Cowichan, the trail crosses the thirty-five-metre-high and ninety-metre-long Marie Canyon trestle over the Cowichan River. After another ten kilometres, the trail crosses another stunning trestle, that which extends for seventy-three metres over the Holt Creek Canyon. Then, thirty-four kilometres from Lake Cowichan, the trail encounters the historic Kinsol Trestle, which at thirty-eight metres high and 187 metres long, is possibly the world's highest surviving wooden trestle. Here, at the Renfrew Road parking lot, the rail trail portion ends.

E&N RAIL TRAIL, VICTORIA TO LANGFORD, 17 KM

At the time of this writing, the tracks of the historic E&N railway from Victoria to Courtenay remained in place and are occasionally used by the Southern Railway of Vancouver. Rather than operating on the actual rail right of way, the newly built E&N Rail Trail parallels the tracks themselves. The seventeen-kilometre paved cycle path connects Victoria, Esquimalt, View Royal, and Langford, and links with the Galloping Goose Trail.

ALL ABOARD

TRAIN RIDES YOU CAN STILL ENJOY

With its stunning scenery, there are few better places in North America than Canada's western mountains to enjoy a train ride. These range from the historic *Canadian*, now operated by VIA Rail, the *Skeena*, another VIA trip, which follows the route of the Grand Trunk Pacific, and the more recent luxury train the *Rocky Mountaineer*, which now offers three scheduled rail tours. Many more local train rides also bring back the long lost era, many of them using the iconic puffing steam locomotives.

VIA Rail's *Canadian*

Once the CPR had pierced the mountain wall of the Rockies, tourists began to flock to the newly opened rail line. Many overnighted in the growing number of mountain hotels, such as the Banff Springs and the Chateau Lake Louise; others were content to enjoy the scenery from the luxury of a lounge car. Even the wife

of Sir John A. Macdonald rode through the mountains on the cowcatcher of a locomotive.

At first, since dining cars were simply too heavy to haul up the steep mountain grades, passengers were ushered off the trains to eat in the dining stations. However, once the steep hills were tamed with the opening of the Spiral Tunnels in 1909 and Connaught Tunnel in 1916, trains no longer needed to stop to allow their passengers to eat, and through service became the norm.

After the Second World War, the popularity of the car began to challenge rail passenger service. To help counter this trend, in 1955 the CPR introduced the sleek new *Canadian* train sets, with their chrome coaches, dome cars, sleepers, and bullet lounge at the rear of the train. The rival Canadian National Railway followed up with what it called the *Super Continental*.

Up until 1990, the *Canadian* began its westbound journey in the east with two segments, departing from Montreal and Toronto respectively and joining up at the CPR station in downtown Sudbury. From there, the train followed the most scenic route in Ontario, that along the Lake Superior shore, before rolling across the Prairies and into the Rockies by way of Banff and Lake Louise. Then, in 1990, the federal government of Brian Mulroney, under a transportation minister named Benoit Bouchard, cut VIA service by half and rerouted the *Canadian* off of the CPR tracks and onto the then-government-owned CNR tracks. While this eliminated the Lake Superior segment, it retained a route through the mountains, albeit through Jasper rather than via the southern route. Since then, the frequency of the service has been further reduced, to twice weekly during the winter and three times weekly in the summer. With this alteration, the *Super Continental* was discontinued entirely.

The mountain scenery begins abruptly west of the magnificent stone station in Jasper. Here, the train enters the Yellowhead Pass, the key route for the Grand Trunk Pacific through the mountains. It glides below Fitzwilliam and Robinson mountains, and then past the highest mountain in the Canadian Rockies, Mount Robson. At Red Pass Junction, the route begins to follow another historic rail route, that created by the Canadian Northern Railway. From here it travels through the wide mountain valley formed by the North Thompson River, which the tracks follow for roughly 260 kilometres to Kamloops and the junction with South Thompson River.

While there are few scheduled stops, the train still offers the opportunity for many whistle stops along the line. Such stops allow local residents and wilderness seekers to flag the train down — today a minimum of twenty-four hours' advanced notice is necessary. Most of the original stations on this portion have long gone. Only that at Valemount remains, relocated to become

a museum. A modern VIA mini-station has replaced the historic old CNoR station at Kamloops North, a massive freight yard that includes storage tracks for the sleek *Rocky Mountaineer* train sets.

The tracks cross the wide North Thompson and follow the river's north bank, crossing back and forth numerous times on long, steel-truss bridges, while the tracks of the CPR follow the opposite banks of the river.

The scenery through this area is decidedly desert-like; it is after all among Canada's driest regions. At Ashcroft, the *Canadian* swings south to follow the steepening canyon of the river. At Lytton, the waters of the Thompson mix with those of the Fraser and enter the dramatic Fraser Canyon, which the route traces all the way to Hope. At Cisco, a short distance south of Lytton, the CN and CP tracks cross the canyon, exchanging river banks with two massive bridges in view of each other.

The trains may pause at the former divisional town of Boston Bar for a crew change, but here the former CNoR station has been moved back from the tracks to house a future museum. Below this point, the route passes the foaming Hells Gate Rapids, one of the most challenging construction points for both the CNoR and CPR.

At Hope, the tracks swing west out of the Fraser Canyon and into a widening vista of farm lands of the lush Fraser River delta. Urban landscapes take over gradually, until the train finally slows to a halt at the grand Pacific Central Station in the east end of downtown Vancouver. Built by the Canadian Northern Railway in 1916, the classical station is one of the finest in the country. Here passengers will file through the grand waiting hall and outside to waiting cabs or relatives.

If there is a downside to this top-ranked train ride, it is that parts of the route through the mountains occur during the overnight hours. VIA's printed schedule has the westbound train running between Jasper and Blue River during the afternoon hours, but from there into Chilliwack the trip occurs overnight. The eastbound train runs in daylight from Kamloops to Jasper. While the scenic Rocky Mountains are visible on both trips, the Fraser Canyon is not.

VIA's Scenic *Skeena*

The *Skeena* (now known as Train 5/6) on the other hand stops overnight in Prince George, allowing for two days running during the day. Between Jasper and Prince Rupert, the *Skeena* follows the tracks laid down by the Grand Trunk Pacific Railway in 1915. While only seven scheduled stops are listed on the route, as many as thirty flag stops are available for local passengers. Like the *Canadian*, the *Skeena* uses chrome coaches, including a dome car and bullet lounge. These came from the discontinued portions of the *Canadian* trains. With its overnight stop in Prince George, it does not require sleepers.

As with the *Canadian*, the *Skeena* enters the Rocky Mountain wall west of Jasper. As it enters the Yellowhead Pass, from the junction between the GTP and the CNoR, the *Skeena* angles northwesterly, passing the little settlement of Dunster, where passengers will see the last of the on-site GTP country stations, now converted to a museum. Two hours from Jasper, the first scheduled stop is at McBride, with its large GTP station, which now functions as an arts centre and tourist information office. Few of VIA's "stations" function in that role any more as agents have been replaced with online ticketing.

For the next four hours, the *Skeena* follows the Fraser River, passing tiny communities such as Penny, whose station is now a railway museum in Prince George, or Willow River, with its lonely general store. Between Dewey and Hansard, the *Skeena* crosses one of the route's longer bridges, that over the Fraser, which is shared with automobile traffic which must stop to allow the train to pass. Early evening sees the *Skeena* cross the long low bridge over the Fraser and through the massive CN yards to the modern Prince George CN station.

For anyone turning back here, or staying a few days, the Railway and Forestry Museum is worth a visit. Most of downtown Prince George is within walking distance of the station.

The following morning, nearly three hours out of Prince George, the *Skeena* may stop at Endako, once a busy CN divisional point, but little remains now to testify to that role, except perhaps the Endako Pub, a former hotel which once housed train crews. Another three hours will bring up the Telkwa Mountains, which, although scenic, do not compare to the majestic Rockies.

Mid-afternoon, the train arrives at Smithers, another of the GTP's divisional points, and still a busy railway spot. The large two-storey station is simpler in concept than that at McBride, but nonetheless historic. From this point, the *Skeena* follows the banks of the Skeena River, where many early settlements arose before tracks were laid. About three hours beyond Smithers, the train will glide past a pair of ghost towns, with the names Dorreen, which still retains its old general store and boxcar sized station, and Pacific, which, despite the bush which thrives here, was once a GTP divisional point where the foundations of the roundhouse may yet be visible.

VIA Rail's Skeena *(now Train 5/6) provides a scenic two-day excursion between Jasper, Alberta, and Prince Rupert, British Columbia. (Photo courtesy VIA Rail Canada.)*

Around 6 p.m., the *Skeena* arrives in the modern community of Terrace, where the building that now serves as the station was once the historic home of the town's founder, George Little.

For the next two hours, the train follows the ever-widening Skeena River, passing First Nations villages as the Kitimat Mountains loom closer. Finally, in the early evening, the *Skeena* pulls up at the modern VIA station that is now part of the BC and Alaska Ferry terminals. The earlier CN station still stands, its ultimate re-use uncertain, farther along the shore. There, in an adjacent park, the Kwinitsa GTP station has been preserved as a museum. The shops and cafes of Cow Bay lie near the waterfront as well.

The Rocky Mountaineer *offers one of North America's most popular train excursions. The scenery shown here is an obvious reason why. (Photo courtesy* Rocky Mountaineer.*)*

Rocky Mountaineer

It may surprise aficionados of the "world's most beautiful train," that the *Rocky Mountaineer* began life as a VIA Rail train. In 1988, VIA introduced the *Rocky Mountaineer* as a scenic, all-daylight tour train for the Jasper to Vancouver route — a trip that, if it was to be made in daylight, required an overnight stop in Kamloops. But with the ill-conceived Bouchard cuts to VIA in 1990, the tour train was offered to the private sector. Recognizing the value of a tour train through Canada's most stunning scenery, the Great Canadian Rail Tour Company leapt into action and acquired the brand.

Its first train departed Vancouver on May 27, 1990, bound for Calgary. They called the route "First Passage to the West," in honour of the CPR main line, Canada's first route to the West Coast.

Since that beginning, the company (later renamed the Armstrong Hospitality Group) added new routes, including "Journey Through the Clouds," which runs from Vancouver to Jasper via Kamloops on the old CNoR main line, taking in the lower Fraser Canyon with the iconic Hells Gate rapids. The "Rainforest to Gold Rush" route follows the line built by the former British Columbia Railway (originally the Pacific Great Eastern). This train departs from the North Vancouver station and may stop at Whistler before overnighting in Quesnel. The route first leads along the dramatic Pacific Coast shoreline, with its soaring cliffs, then passes through the dark canyons of the Coast Range into the gold rush country of Lillooet. Crossing the massive bridge over the Fraser River, it enters the desert-like Fraser River Canyon. At Prince George, the route switches onto the tracks of the former GTP, passing through McBride beneath the looming peak on Mount Robson, the highest peak of the Rockies. The "Coastal Passage" is the company's first cross border experience, offering passengers the chance to ride its trains along the Pacific Coast from Vancouver to Seattle.

The *Rocky Mountaineer* offers a three-day itinerary, known as the "Circle Journey," that begins in Jasper and includes overnight stops in Kamloops and Vancouver. The current version of "First Passage to the West" includes a choice of a two-day return journey to Lake Louise or to Banff, or a three-day journey with overnight stops in Kamloops and Banff.

The company can now boast of seventy coaches, most of which were built originally in the 1950s and formerly operated on CN's former transcontinental routes. These were rebuilt for the Redleaf and Silverleaf level of service. In the 1990s, the company introduced its dome cars — each with full-length domes and its own kitchen galley. These are for the luxury Goldleaf level of service. With its stunning scenery, its high quality of on-board service and fine-dining experience, the *Rocky Mountaineer* has often been named "The World's Leading Travel Experience by Train." And no doubt it will be again.

The train's station locations include North Vancouver on Philip Avenue, Banff, Jasper, Lake Louise, Calgary, Whistler, Quesnel, Kamloops, and Seattle. The main Vancouver station lies a block from Terminal Avenue, in a renovated CN car shop, a short distance east of the grand Pacific Central station, home to VIA and Amtrak.

Royal Canadian Pacific

If there is any rail experience that is more luxurious (or exclusive) than the *Rocky Mountaineer*, it is that offered by the CPR's *Royal Canadian Pacific* tour train. Built at the CPR's Montreal shops, these historic coaches were not for ordinary passengers, but rather for CPR executives, favoured politicians, and visiting royalty.

The *Banffshire*, built in 1926, and the *N.R. Crump* (1930) provide luxurious sleeping accommodations. The *Strathcona, the Van Horne*, and the *Royal Wentworth* are all business cars, built in the 1920s and containing lounges, dining facilities, and staterooms. The *Craigellachie* offers both sleeping and fine dining, while the grandest of the set would be the *Mount Stephen* car. Named for the CPR's first president, and built for the director, it contains the iconic rear vestibule so often seen in railway photographs.

The visiting dignitaries who have ridden in these cars include King George VI with Queen Elizabeth (the Queen Mother), Queen Elizabeth II and the Duke of Edinburgh, as well as prominent politicians like Winston Churchill, F.D. Roosevelt, and Prime Minister Mackenzie King. With its meals and accommodation, the *Royal Canadian Pacific* is a five-star resort on wheels. Tours can include the single-day "Banff Dinner Train," or multi-day excursions from Calgary to Vancouver along the CPR's historic main-line route. The "Rockies Experience" follows a circle route from Calgary, to Golden, Fernie, and Lethbridge, before heading back into Calgary. Fishing and golfing excursions are also available.

There is no scheduled public service and bookings are normally available to private charters only. Departures are from the historic CPR Palliser Hotel in downtown Calgary. Pertinent information is on the company's website, www.royalcanadianpacific.com.

Burnaby Central Electric Railway, Burnaby, B.C.

Situated in Burnaby's Confederation Park, the BCER (not to be confused with the British Columbia Electric Railway) traces its origins to 1929, when a group of miniature railway enthusiasts organized themselves into a club, which operated its train sets in its members' yards. In 1975, the club had moved its operations to the Burnaby Village Museum before ultimately relocating to a more spacious, seven-acre site, once used as a municipal works yard. Here they laid down more than three kilometres of "main-line" tracks, which wound its way around "mountains," through tunnels, and under bridges. Trains depart from an authentic-looking, two-storey train station. From there, visitors can clamber onto open coaches behind engines built to resemble steam, diesel, or electric locomotives, all representing a different era in railway history. The park is situated at the corner of Willoughby and Penzance drives, just three kilometres from Highway 1 at Exit 29.

Kamloops Heritage Railway, Kamloops, B.C.

Nothing evokes Canada's railway heritage like a steam locomotive. In 1994, the KHR Society came to life to acquire and restore the CNR's steam locomotive #2141. This large, 2-8-0 engine was built for the Canadian Northern Railway in 1910 and operated until 1958, when it was replaced with diesel. In 2002, the City of Kamloops, recognizing the value of its railway roots, offered the society funds and a loan as well as a building to house the

The railway museum in Kamloops, British Columbia, has preserved historic railway equipment as part of its steam train excursions.

locomotive and the organization's growing collection of rolling stock. In June of 2002, #2141 got up its head of steam and carried its first passengers from the Kamloops CN station across the bridge over the South Thompson River. That first year alone more than ninety-five thousand visitors enjoyed a return to rails' early days.

The *Spirit of Kamloops* offers summer excursions, which last one and a half hours. A "ghost train" offers Hallowe'en trips, while the *Spirit of Christmas* celebrates the Yuletide season for four days over the weekend prior to Christmas. The trains depart from the historic CN Kamloops station, which is now a restaurant. The ticket office is in a more modern building, behind the old station. Two baggage cars and a 1930 coach, as well as various examples of other rolling stock, are housed in the society's shops beside Pioneer Park in Kamloops. These premises are not currently open to the public as a museum. Its excursion train may haul two open coaches as well as a 1954 CN coach, and a 1954 café lounge.

Kimberley's Underground Mining Railway, Kimberley, B.C.

Given the mining history of the area and of the famous Sullivan Mine, it is fitting that the Kimberley Underground Railway would appear. The vision began in 1978, when the Sullivan Mine and Railway Historical Society was formed with the notion of creating a commuter line from downtown Kimberley to a nearby ski hill. By 1984, it was operating a two-and-a-half-kilometre route around the Happy Hans Campground. In 1994, it was extended to Kimberley's "downtown" station, and a decade later to the Alpine Resort. In 2005, a 750-metre tunnel was drilled in Mark Creek Valley to house the Sullivan Mine interpretive centre. Not only does the route take in the valley scenery but it also includes a stop at the mine interpretive centre in the tunnel as well as at the Sullivan Mine powerhouse. Trains depart from the new station situated just off Gerry Sorensen Way west of the downtown Paltzi pedestrian mall.

Alberni Pacific Railway, Port Alberni, B.C.

This steam train operates between the restored Port Alberni train station, a two-storey CPR structure styled after that in Courtenay, and the McClean Mill National Historic Site about eight kilometres away. The Baldwin 2-8-2 steam locomotive puffs away from the former E&N station on Argyle Street near the waterfront, passing the extensive Western Forest Products plant for a thirty-five-minute excursion through the woods to the McLean Mill.

The mill operated from 1929 to 1965 and two decades later was declared a National Historic Site. It has been undergoing further restoration and is a rare surviving example of a steam-powered mill.

Kettle Valley Steam Railway, Summerland, B.C.

Located on the west side of Okanagan Lake, north of Penticton near the town of Summerland, the Kettle Valley Steam Railway is one of the western mountain's more popular rail tours, following the last remaining trackage of the legendary Kettle Valley Railway.

In 1999, the Prairie Valley station opened to offer rides along the winding scenic tracks to the Canyon View station at Trout Creek, where a bridge soars more than seventy metres above the water below. It is said to be the third-largest of its kind in North America. The ninety-minute round trip is hauled by a 2-8-0 CP steam locomotive, #3716, originally built in 1912 and known today as the *Spirit of Summerland*. Alternative motive power might include an ALCO S-6 diesel locomotive. Passengers ride in open coaches or in one of three former CP coaches built circa 1950. These may also be used for special trips. The track curves high above the rolling valleys of the Okanagan, where a specially staged "train robbery" might await unsuspecting passengers. The train operates regularly through the summer, and on special occasions throughout the rest of the year.

East Kootenay Railway, Fort Steele, B.C.

From the restored ghost town of Fort Steele, which the CPR bypassed as a divisional town, a 1926 2-6-2 former logging locomotive hauls visitors on a short twenty-minute ride through the countryside around the provincial heritage town, stopping at the Kootenay River lookout. The trackage is the railway's own, and not any part of the old CPR route.

Steamer 3716 offers scenic steam excursions along the Okanagan Valley at Summerland, British Columbia.

BC Forest Discovery Centre

The steam locomotive collection began here in the 1950s, when Gerry Wellburn got his hands on a 1911 Shay logging locomotive from MacMillan Bloedel. The collection grew to nearly ten locomotives, one of which, the 1910 *Samson*, leads visitors on a 2.5-kilometre tour around the museum grounds, including over the wooden Somenos Lake trestle. Although the steam locomotive runs only on summer, weekend riders can at other times enjoy the Green Hornet gas locomotive.

Nelson Street Railway, Nelson, B.C.

Before intensive lobbying by the automobile, gasoline, and rubber-tire interests ended their service, streetcars served nearly every major community in North America. This was certainly the case in Nelson B.C.. From 1925 to 1949, streetcars rumbled along the streets of this former boom town. Today, that history is recalled with the restoration of Streetcar #23 by the Nelson Electric Tramway Streetcar Society. Since its inauguration in 1992, the summer excursion follows a track along the shore of scenic Kootenay Lake from its two-stall car barn to the door of the Prestige Lake Resort and Conference Centre.

Kaoham Shuttle, Lillooet, B.C.

When BC Rail ended its vital rail passenger service into British Columbia's interior, the Seton First Nation took over a short portion of the line from Seton Portage to Lillooet. The train servicing this route returns the same day, with a stop at Shalalth. This one-hour trip offers more than just an opportunity to do the shopping for the First Nations inhabitants along the line. It provides what is considered by many to be one of North America's most scenic sections of rail line. From Lillooet, it enters the precipitous Seton River Canyon before coming to the shores of the fjord-like Seton Lake, which is abutted by steep granite cliffs that soar two thousand metres above the green waters. Along the way the train also runs through a 1,200 metre tunnel.

Started in 2002, with the end of BC Rail's passenger service, the two-coach "rail bus" follows tracks laid down in 1915 by the Pacific Great Eastern Railway (which later became BC Rail and is now CN Rail). In the local St'at'imc language, Kaoham means "to meet the train." With two return trips on Fridays, travellers can depart Lillooet and return later in the day. As a result the shuttle has become a popular draw for tourists and rail excursionists.

COMMUTER TRAINS

SkyTrain, Vancouver, B.C.

Few tourists look upon commuter rail travel as offering potential tours. Yet, riding on either Vancouver's SkyTrain or the interurban West Coast Express can provide a cross-section of a variety of urban landscapes. Inspired by Expo 86, a transportation showcase, the SkyTrain inaugurated its first run on January of that year. The "Expo" Line, as it was called, expanded from twenty-one kilometres to twenty-nine kilometres by 1994, and had twenty stations. The Millennium Line opened in 1995 and in just a little over a decade had grown to twenty kilometres. The third leg was the Canada Line, which linked the City of Vancouver with Richmond and with the international airport as well. Another segment, the Evergreen Line, is slated to open in 2016.

The SkyTrain routes operate mostly above ground, offering travellers views of historic streetscapes, heritage buildings, and watery vistas from atop high bridges. SkyTrain service is frequent, inexpensive and offers day passes.

West Coast Express, Vancouver to Mission City, B.C.

The West Coast Express runs five daily trains between Mission City and the former CP station on Vancouver's waterfront, a distance of sixty kilometres. The disadvantage is that the only west-bound trains are the morning commuter trains, and it is the reverse in the evening, so it becomes difficult to make a day trip of it.

Even Vancouver's SkyTrain, although part of the city's public transit system, offers interesting viewing opportunities of the city.

COME AND GONE

Pacific Wilderness Railway, Vancouver Island

Not all tour train operations have succeeded. One such case was the short-lived Pacific Wilderness Train. It began operations in June of 2000 to take tourists from downtown Victoria to the scenic heights of Malahat, a distance of thirty kilometres. Three GP-10 diesels, painted in the CPR colours of maroon and gold, and leased from the Ohio Central Railroad, hauled three vintage coaches similarly painted up. Despite the efforts of local residents and businesses to create a tour train operation, in 2001 it was attracting only ninety passengers a day. When the hoped-for steam engines failed to show up the line ceased operation.

Okanagan Valley Wine Train

Another example of CN's indifference to Canada's railway heritage is its treatment of the marooned coaches from the Okanagan Valley Wine Train. This five-hour scenic tour of the wine region of the Okanagan Valley from Kelowna to Vernon operated only from 1998 to 2002. The train offered theme coaches, dining, entertainment, and overnight accommodation as a bed and breakfast.

The blue-and-gold VIA coaches, built originally by the CNR in the 1950s, originated as part of the doomed *Super Continental* cross-country train. Following their last departure in 2002, the coaches remained isolated on an industrial siding in Kelowna, waiting for CN to remove them to an alternative location. But in 2014 CN abandoned the line from Kelowna to Vernon and prepared to lift the tracks, a move that would have stranded the coaches with no way out, other than by truck. Fortunately, this story has a happy ending. In 2015, the train set was purchased by the Aspen Crossing railway attraction in southern Alberta, adding to that site's growing roster of heritage rail cars and train excursions. And so, thanks once more to the love Canadians have for their railway heritage, that heritage lives on. All aboard!

SOME RAILWAY MISCELLANEA

THE WHEELS

The numbers 2-8-0 et cetera appear with steam locomotives. These refer to the wheel configuration. For example, "2-8-0" would mean that the locomotive has two small wheels at the front of the locomotive, eight large one in the middle, which drive the engine, and none at the rear in this case. Other configurations might be 0-4-0, which would be typical for the smaller locomotives, of the type usually used for mining operations, or 4-8-4, which would have been typical of the larger cross country steam engines.

THE GAUGES

Tracks were built to different widths, known as gauges. Today's standard North American gauge is 4' 8½". This width derives from ancient Roman times, when that was the width of chariot wheels and also the general width of a team of two horses. That simply carried on to stage coach widths and those of the railways wheels as well. While a wider gauge was tried, it proved cumbersome. Narrow gauge was normally 3'6" and was used on some main-line operations, until company amalgamations stipulated that the gauges be standardized. Mining operations often still use the narrow gauge or even one of 2'4".

THE GRADES

To operate effectively, railway grades could be no more than 2.2 percent, or a rise of 2.2 feet over 100 feet of track. The early mountain grades of 4.5 percent, which is what the CPR encountered in the Big Hill, near Field, proved too difficult for the early steam engines. These were lowered as soon as tunnels like the Spiral Tunnels and the Connaught Tunnels could replace them.

THE GALLOPING GOOSE

What on earth is a "galloping goose"? It is a self-propelled rail car, which somewhat resembles a school bus on train wheels, with seating for passengers near the front and a higher freight section at the rear. With few passengers on this route, this single car coach was more economical to run than a full train. There are a few which run as tour operations in the United States.

BIBLIOGRAPHY

BOOKS, ARTICLES, AND PAMPHLETS

Adair, Daryl T. *Canadian Rail Travel Guide*. Markham, ON: Fitzhenry and Whiteside, 2004.

Andreae, Christopher. *Lines of Country: An Atlas of Railway and Waterway History in Canada*. Erin, ON: Boston Mills Press, 1997.

Argyle, Ray. *The Boy in the Picture: The Craigellachie Kid and the Driving of the Last Spike*. Toronto: Dundurn Press, 2010.

Baird, Ian. *CPR Railway Stations in BC*. Victoria: Orca Book Publishers, 1990.

———. *A Historical Guide to the E&N Railway*. Victoria: Friends of the E&N, 1985

Ballantyne, Bruce, ed. *Canadian Railway Station Guide*. Ottawa: Bytown Railway Society Inc., 1998.

Bohi, Charles W. *Canadian National's Western Depots*. Markham, ON: Fitzhenry and Whiteside, 2002.

Bohi, Charles W. and Leslie S. Kozma. *Canadian Pacific's Western Depots*. David City, NE: South Platte Press, 1994.

Brown, Ron. *The Train Doesn't Stop Here Anymore: An Illustrated History of the Railway Station in Canada*. Toronto: Dundurn Press, 2013.

Burrows, Roger C. *Railway Mileposts: British Columbia, Volume I, the CPR Mainline Route*. North Vancouver: Railway Milepost Books, 1984.

———. *Railway Mileposts British Columbia, Volume II, The Southern Route*. North Vancouver: Railway Milepost Books, 1984.

Bush, E.F. *Engine Houses and Turntables in Canada, 1850–1950*. Erin, ON: Boston Mills Press, 1999.

Cooper, Bruce Clement. *The Golden Age of Canadian Railways*. Stroud, Glouchestershire, UK: Bookcraft, 2010.

Davies, David and Lorne Nicklason. *The CPR's English Bay Branch*. Vancouver: Canadian Railway Historical Association, West Coast Division, 1993.

Fernie and District Historical Society. *Heritage Walking Tour*. nd.

Langford, Dan. *Cycling the KVR*. Calgary: Rocky Mountain Books, 2002.

Martin, J. Edward. *Railway Stations of Western Canada: An Architectural History*. White Rock, BC: Studio E, 1980.

Mika, Nick and Helma Mika, with Donald M. Wilson. *Canada's Railways*. Belleville, ON: Mika Publishing, 1986.

Murray, Tom. *Rails Across Canada: History of the Canadian Pacific and Canadian National Railways*. nd.

Obee, Bruce. *Trans Canada Trail: British Columbia*. Vancouver: Whitecap Books, 2008.

Roberts, Erle W. and David P. Stremes, eds. *Canadian Trackside Guide 2014*. Ottawa: Bytown Railway Society, 2014.

Robinson, Bart. *Banff Springs: The Story of a Hotel*. Banff: Summerthought Publishing, 2007.

Sanford, Barrie, *McCulloch's Wonder*. Vancouver: Whitecap Books, 1977.

Solomon, Briand. *North American Railroad Bridges*. Saint Paul, MN: MBI Publishing Company and Voyageur Press, 2007.

Smuin, Joe. *Kettle Valley Railway Mileboards: A Historical Field Guide to the KVR*. nd.

VIA Rail Canada. *Rails Across Canada: 150 Years of Rail Passenger Service in Canada*. Montreal: VIA Rail Canada, 1986.

West Coast Railway Heritage Park Official Souvenir Guide. nd.

White, John. *Driving the KVR*. Winnipeg: North Kildonan Publications, 2003.

WEBSITES

"About Field." *Field, British Columbia*. Last modified 2016. www.field.ca/about.

Agassiz-Harrison Museum and Visitor Information Centre. "About the Museum." Last modified 2011. www.agassizharrisonmuseum.org/index.php/museum.

Banff Heritage Tourism. "Cultural Heritage Tour of Lake Louise: Self Guided." www.crmr.com/wp/wp-content/uploads/2012/07/Lake-Louise-Heritage-Building-Brochure-2011.pdf.

BC Forest Discovery Centre. bcforestdiscoverycentre.com.

"British Columbia Electric Railway." *Wikipedia*. Last modified January 29, 2016. en.wikipedia.org/wiki/British_Columbia_Electric_Railway.

Burnaby Central Railway. burnabyrailway.org.

Canadian Museum of Rail Travel. *TrainsDeluxe*. Last modified April 26, 2013. www.trainsdeluxe.com.

"Canadian Pacific Railway District Superintendent's House - Nelson, BC." *Waymarking*. Last modified 2016. www.waymarking.com/waymarks/WMH8GX_Canadian_Pacific_Railway_District_Superintendents_House_Nelson_BC.

Canadian Railroad Historical Association Esquimalt & Nanaimo Division. Last modified 2016. www.encrha.com.

Canadian Railway Hall of Fame. Last modified 2006. www.railfame.ca.

"Cisco Bridges." *Wikipedia*. Last modified January 12, 2016. en.wikipedia.org/wiki/Cisco_Bridges.

City of Port Moody. "Port Moody Station Museum." *Port Moody: City of the Arts*. Last modified 2016. www.portmoody. ca/index.aspx?page=79.

"Cowichan Valley Regional Trail." *Trans Canada Trail*. tctrail.ca/about-the-trail/featured-trails/cowichan-valley-trail-kinsol-trestle-b-c.

"CPR Railway Water Tower - Port Alberni, BC." *Waymarking*. Last modified 2016. www.waymarking.com/waymarks/WM9ARH_CPR_Railway_Water_Tower_Port_Alberni_BC.

Critchley, Darren. "Othello Tunnels." *Touring the Kettle Valley Railway*. Last modified 2016. www.thekvr.com/othello.php.

Destination BC Corp. "Cariboo Chilcotin Coast: Railway History." *Super, Natural British Columbia*. Last modified 2015. www.hellobc.com/cariboo-chilcotin-coast/culture-history/railway-history.aspx.

District Of Lillooet. "Historical Sites." *Lillooet*. Last modified 2016. lillooetbc.ca/Arts,-Culture-Community/Historical-Sites.aspx.

"E&N Railway's Victoria Roundhouse." *Canadian Railroad Historical Association Esquimalt & Nanaimo Division*. www.encrha.com/roundhouse.php.

Eagland, Nick. "Got a Dollar? Historic Railway Houses the Ultimate Fixer-Up Projects: 100-Year-Old Houses Stand Empty in Fraser River Town of North Bend." *Province*. October 25, 2015. www.theprovince.com/travel/dollar+historic+railway+houses+ultimate+fixer+projects/11466772/story.html.

Elder, Jeff. "Railway Bridge an Iconic Piece of Local History." *Prince George Citizen*. June 16, 2014. www.princegeorge-citizen.com/news/local-news/railway-bridge-an-iconic-piece-of-local-history-1.1131336.

Fort Steele. "Museum & Heritage Buildings." *Fort Steele Heritage Town*. Last modified 2016. fortsteele.ca/attractions/buildings.

Forth Junction Heritage Society. "Western Canada's Largest Railway Bridges." *Forth Junction Project*. Last modified November 2014. forthjunction.ca/railway-bridges-canadawest.htm.

Fraser Valley Heritage Railway Society. "Our History." *Surrey's Heritage Rail*. Last modified 2015. fvhrs.org/history.

"Freeport." *The British Columbia Folklore Society*. Last modified 2016. folklore.bc.ca/freeport.

Galloping Goose Trail. www.gallopinggoosetrail.com.

"The Grand Trunk Pacific Railway 100 years in the Skeena Valley." *Regional Disctrict of Kitimat-Stikine*. www.rdks.bc.ca/content/grand-trunk-pacific-railway-skeena-valley.

Hatley Castle. Last modified 2016. www.hatleycastle.com.

"The History of Quilchena Ranch." *Douglas Lake Ranch*. Last modified 2014. www.douglaslake.com/history-quilchena.html.

"History of SkyTrain." *TransLink*. Last modified 2016. www.translink.ca/en/About-Us/Corporate- Overview/Operating-Companies/BCRTC/History- of-SkyTrain.aspx.

"How to Get There." *Galloping Goose Trail*. www.gallopinggoosetrail.com/map_galloping_goose_directions.html#.

Interactive Broadcasting Corporation. "The Kettle Valley Railway Trails." *British Columbia's Travel Guide.* Last modified 2015. www.bcadventure.com/adventure/explore/ok/trails/kettle.htm.

International Selkirk Loop. "Sandon." *The International Selkirk Loop.* Last modified 2016. selkirkloop.org/index.php/travel/cities/British-Columbia/Sandon.html.

The Iredale Partnership. "Report on Short-Term, Long-Term Potential of the Cranbrook CP Rail Roundhouse." March, 1989. www.crowsnest.bc.ca/cmrt/roundhouse-study.pdf.

"Kamloops CN Railway Bridge." *HistoricBridges.org.* Last modified 2016. historicbridges.org/bridges/browser/?bridgebrowser=britishcolumbia/kamloopsrr.

Kimberley's Sullivan Mine & Historical Society. *Kimberley's Underground Mining Railway.* Last modified 2007. www.kimberleysundergroundminingrailway.ca/activities.php?pID=13.

"Kinsol Trestle." *Wikipedia.* Last modified August 11, 2015. https://en.wikipedia.org/wiki/Kinsol_Trestle.

Kluckner, Michael. "The North Bend Store and CPR Buildings." *Michael Kluckner.* www.michaelkluckner.com/bciw6nbstore.html.

"The Laurel Packinghouse." *Kelowna Museums.* Last modified 2015. https://www.kelownamuseums.ca/museums/the-laurel-packinghouse.

MacDonald, John. "Canadian Railway Tunnels and Snow Sheds." *Old Canadian Railways.* yourrailwaypictures.com/Tunnels.

McCubbin, Gail. *The McCubbins of Pacific.* www.themccubbins.com.

"Myra Canyon Trestles (2006)." *Canadian Railway Hall of Fame.* Last modified 2006. www.railfame.ca/sec_ind/technology/en_2006_MyraCanyon Trestles.asp.

The Nelson Electric Tramway Society. www.nelsonstreetcar.org.

"New Westminster Bridge." *Wikipedia.* Last modified March 11, 2016. https://en.wikipedia.org/wikiNew_Westminster_Bridge.

"New Westminster Railway Bridge." *HistoricalBridges.org.* Last modified 2016. historicbridges.org/bridges/browser/?bridgebrowser=britishcolumbia/newwestminsterrailwaybridge.

Newman, Ken. "First Train." *Terrace Standard.* April 8, 2014. www.terracestandard.com/news/254053391.html.

The Old City Quarter Association. "Occidental Hotel." *Old City Quarter Nanaimo.* Last modified 2013. www.oldcity-quarter.com/tour/occidental.htm.

Pearson, Jim A. *British Columbia Grain Elevators.* vanishingalberta.ca/B.C._Elevators.html.

"Prince George Railway Bridge." *Historicbridges.org.* Last modified 2016. historicbridges.org/bridges/browser/?bridgebrowser=britishcolumbia/grandtrunkpacific.

Province of British Columbia. "Coquihalla Canyon Provincial Park." *BC Parks.* Last modified 2016. www.env.gov.bc.ca/bcparks/explore/parkpgs/coquihalla_cyn.

"Railway Tunnels in Canada > 500 m." *The World's Longest Tunnel Page.* Last modified January 4, 2007. www.lotsberg.net/data/canada/rail.html.

"Railways on Vancouver Island – Photos and Discussion." *West Coast Ferries Forum.* ferriesbc.proboards.com/thread/8911/railways-vancouver-island-photos-discussion?page=3.

"Rich History at Former Rail Settlements." *Terrace Standard.* April 9, 2014. www.terracestandard.com/news/254053451.html.

"Rogers Pass National Historic Site of Canada." *Parks Canada.* Last modified February 24, 2014. www.pc.gc.ca/eng/lhn-nhs/bc/rogers/natcul/natcul1.aspx.

Sandon Museum. Last modified 2016. www.sandonmuseum.ca.

"Stoney Creek Bridge." *Wikipedia.* Last modified Feraury 12, 2016. https://en.wikipedia.org/wiki/Stoney_Creek_Bridge.

The Ties that Bind: Building the CPR, Building a Place in Canada. Last modified 2010. www.mhso.ca/tiesthatbind/.

Tourism Surrey. "Fraser Valley Heritage Railway Society." *Surrey.* Last modified 2016. www.tourismsurrey.com/partners/do-see/fraser-valley-heritage-railway-society.

The Trails Society of British Columbia. "Spur: Great Northern Rail Trail (Salmo to Nelson)." *Trails B.C.* Last modified 2014. trailsbc.ca/tct/west-kootenay/spur-salmo.

Valemount Museum. *Valemount, British Columbia History and Historic Railway Station.* Last modified 2016. valemountmuseum.ca.

VIA Rail Canada, Inc. "VIA Rail an Astounding History." *VIA Rail Canada.* Last modified 2016. www.viarail.ca/en/about-via-rail/our-company/our-history/via-rail-astounding-history.

Volovsek, Walter. "Columbia & Western Railway (Boundary Rail Trail)." *Trails in Time.* Last modified 2016. www.trailsintime.org/html/columbiawestern.

"Yoho National Park." *Parks Canada.* Last modified April 16, 2014. www.pc.gc.ca/eng/pn-np/bc/yoho/natcul/spirale-spiral.aspx.

INDEX

Rails to the Atlantic

Follow *Rails to the Atlantic* through eastern Canada's railway heritage. Visit preserved railway stations in various states of use, or take in the architecture of the grand era of station building in Quebec City, Halifax, and St. John's. Board scenic railway excursions on the Orford Express or Le Train du Massif de Charlevoix, or travel to VIA Rail's destinations in remote northern Quebec.

Rail trails lead through the Laurentian mountains and Quebec's Eastern Townships. Museums exhibit Newfoundland's colourful railway heritage, while Canada's largest railway equipment display lies near Montreal. Magnificent railway hotels include the Fairmont Le Chateau Montebello and the Algonquin Resort, as well as the stunning Chateau-style station hotel at McAdam, New Brunswick. Often forgotten are the railway bridges and trestles, stunning feats of engineering that stretch across wide valleys and churning rivers, the construction of which sometimes led to deadly consequences. Lesser-known attractions, such as roundhouses and employee housing, are profiled to help bring the railway era back to life.

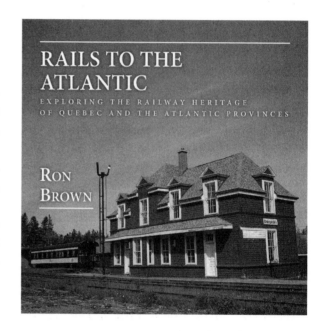

RAILS TO THE
ATLANTIC
EXPLORING THE RAILWAY HERITAGE
OF QUEBEC AND THE ATLANTIC PROVINCES

RON
BROWN

Rails Across the Prairies

Rails Across the Prairies traces the evolution of Canada's rail network, including the appearance of the first steam engine on the back of a barge. The book looks at the arrival of European settlers before the railway and examines how they coped by using ferry services on the Assiniboine and North Saskatchewan Rivers. The work then follows the building of the railways, the rivalries of their owners, and the unusual irrigation works of Canadian Pacific Railway. The towns were nearly all the creation of the railways from their layout to their often unusual names.

Eventually, the rail lines declined, though many are experiencing a limited revival. Learn what the heritage lover can still see of the Prairies' railway legacy, including existing rail operations and the stories the railways brought with them. Many landmarks lie vacant, including ghost towns and elevators, while many others survive as museums or interpretative sites.

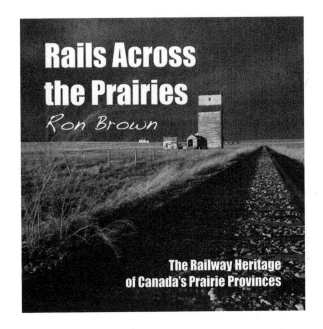

Available at your favourite bookseller

VISIT US AT
Dundurn.com
@dundurnpress
Facebook.com/dundurnpress
Pinterest.com/dundurnpress